THE VERTEX COLORING ALGORITHM

ASHAY DHARWADKER

ABSTRACT

We present a new polynomial-time algorithm for finding proper m-colorings of the vertices of a graph. We prove that every graph with n vertices and maximum vertex degree Δ must have chromatic number $\chi(G)$ less than or equal to $\Delta+1$ and that the algorithm will always find a proper m-coloring of the vertices of G with m less than or equal to $\Delta+1$. Furthermore, we prove that this condition is the best possible in terms of n and Δ by explicitly constructing graphs for which the chromatic number is exactly $\Delta+1$. In the special case when G is a connected simple graph and is neither an odd cycle nor a complete graph, we show that the algorithm will always find a proper m-coloring of the vertices of G with m less than or equal to Δ. In the process, we obtain a new constructive proof of Brooks' famous theorem of 1941. For all known examples of graphs, the algorithm finds a proper m-coloring of the vertices of the graph G for m equal to the chromatic number $\chi(G)$. In view of the importance of the **P** versus **NP** question, we ask: *does there exist a graph G for which this algorithm cannot find a proper m-coloring of the vertices of G with m equal to the chromatic number $\chi(G)$?* The algorithm is demonstrated with several examples of famous graphs, including a proper four-coloring of the map of India and two large Mycielski benchmark graphs with hidden minimum vertex colorings. We implement the algorithm in C++ and provide a demonstration program for Microsoft Windows.

The Demonstration Program

http://www.dharwadker.org/vertex_coloring

CONTENTS

1. Introduction

In 1972, Karp [1] introduced a list of twenty-one **NP**-complete problems, one of which was the problem of trying to find a proper m-coloring of the vertices of a graph, where m is a fixed integer greater than 2. Given a graph and a set of m colors, one must find out if it is possible to assign a color to each vertex such that no two adjacent vertices are assigned the same color. Such an assignment is called a proper m-coloring of the vertices of a graph. Even if such a coloring exists, it can be very difficult to find in general. For example, try to find a proper 3-coloring of the vertices of the Frucht graph [2] shown below in Figure 1.1.

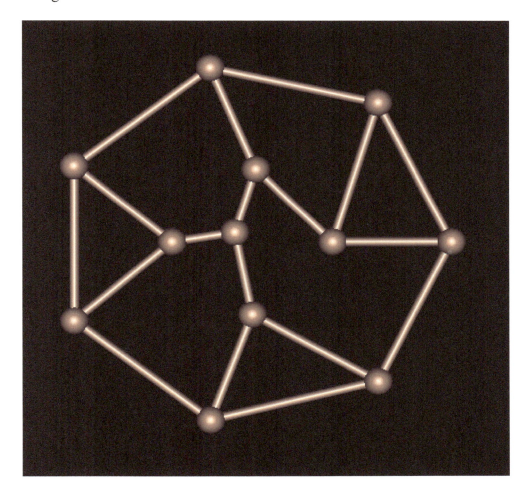

Figure 1.1. *Find a proper 3-coloring of the vertices*

We present a new polynomial-time **VERTEX COLORING ALGORITHM** for finding proper m-colorings of the vertices of a graph. In Section 2, we provide precise **DEFINITIONS** of all the terminology used. In Section 3, we present a formal description of the **ALGORITHM** followed by a small example to show how the algorithm works step-by-step. In Section 4, we show that the algorithm has polynomial-time **COMPLEXITY**. In Section 5, we establish conditions of **SUFFICIENCY** for a graph to have a proper m-coloring. We prove that every graph with n vertices and maximum vertex degree Δ must have chromatic number $\chi(G)$ less than or equal to $\Delta+1$ and that the algorithm will always find a proper m-coloring of the vertices of G with m less than or equal to $\Delta+1$. Furthermore, we prove that this condition is the best possible in terms of n and Δ by explicitly constructing graphs for which the chromatic number is exactly $\Delta+1$. In the special case when G is a connected simple graph and is neither an odd cycle nor a complete graph, we show that the algorithm will always find a proper m-coloring of the vertices of G with m less than or equal to Δ. In the process, we obtain a new constructive proof of Brooks' famous theorem of 1941. For all known examples of graphs, the algorithm finds a proper m-coloring of the vertices of the graph G for m equal to the chromatic number $\chi(G)$. In view of the importance of the **P** versus **NP** question **[3]**, we ask: *does there exist a graph G for which this algorithm cannot find a proper m-coloring of the vertices of G with m equal to the chromatic number $\chi(G)$?* In Section 6, we provide an **IMPLEMENTATION** of the algorithm as a C++ program, together with demonstration software for Microsoft Windows. In Section 7, we demonstrate the algorithm with several **EXAMPLES** of famous graphs, including a proper four-coloring of the map of India and two large Mycielski benchmark graphs with hidden minimum vertex colorings. In Section 8, we list the **REFERENCES**.

2. Definitions

We begin with precise definitions of all the terminology and notation used in this presentation, following **[4]**. We use the usual notation $\lfloor x \rfloor$ to denote the *floor function* i.e. the greatest integer not greater than x and $\lceil x \rceil$ to denote the *ceiling function* i.e. the least integer not less than x.

A *simple graph G* with n vertices consists of a set of *vertices V*, with $|V| = n$, and a set of *edges E*, such that each edge is an unordered pair of distinct vertices. Note that the definition of G explicitly forbids *loops* (edges joining a vertex to itself) and *multiple edges* (many edges joining a pair of vertices), whence the set E must also be finite. We may *label* the vertices of G with the integers $1, 2, \ldots, n$. If the unordered pair of vertices $\{u, v\}$ is an edge in G, we say that u is a *neighbor* of v (or u is *adjacent* to v) and write $uv \in E$. Neighborhood is clearly a symmetric relationship: $uv \in E$ if and only if $vu \in E$. The *degree* of a vertex v, denoted by $d(v)$, is the number of neighbors of v. The *maximum degree* over all vertices of G is denoted by Δ. The *adjacency matrix* of G is an $n \times n$ matrix with the entry in row u and column v equal to 1 if $uv \in E$ and equal to 0 otherwise. Given graphs G and H, the *Cartesian product G×H* is defined as the graph whose set of vertices is $V(G) \times V(H)$ with an edge connecting vertex (u_1, v_1) with vertex (u_2, v_2) if and only if either $u_1 = u_2$ and $\{v_1, v_2\}$ is an edge in H or $v_1 = v_2$ and $\{u_1, u_2\}$ is an edge in G. A *clique Q* of a graph G is a subset of vertices such that every unordered pair of vertices in Q is an edge. If all the vertices of a graph form a clique then the graph is said to be *complete*. A complete graph with m vertices is denoted by K_m. An *independent set S* of a graph G is a set of vertices such that no unordered pair of vertices in S is an edge. Given an independent set S of G and a vertex v outside S, we say that v is *adjoinable* if the set

$S \cup \{v\}$ is still an independent set of G. Denote by $\rho(S)$ the *number of adjoinable vertices* of an independent set S of G. A *maximal independent set* has no adjoinable vertices. A *maximum independent set* is an independent set with the largest number of vertices. Note that a maximum independent set is always maximal but not necessarily vice versa. Given a set of m colors $\{1, 2, ..., m\}$, a *proper m-coloring* of the vertices of a graph G is an assignment of a unique color to each vertex of G such that no two adjacent vertices are assigned the same color. The *chromatic number* $\chi(G)$ of a graph G is the minimum value of m for which there exists a a proper m-coloring of the vertices of G.

An *algorithm* is a problem-solving method suitable for implementation as a computer program. While designing algorithms we are typically faced with a number of different approaches. For small problems, it hardly matters which approach we use, as long as it is one that solves the problem correctly. However, there are many problems for which the only known algorithms take so long to compute the solution that they are practically useless. A *polynomial-time algorithm* is one whose number of computational steps is always bounded by a polynomial function of the size of the input. Thus, a polynomial-time algorithm is one that is actually useful in practice. The class of all such problems that have polynomial-time algorithms is denoted by **P**. For some problems, there are no known polynomial-time algorithms but these problems do have *nondeterministic polynomial-time algorithms*: try all candidates for solutions simultaneously and for each given candidate, verify whether it is a correct solution in polynomial-time. The class of all such problems is denoted by **NP**. Clearly **P** $\subseteq$ **NP**. On the other hand, there are problems that are known to be in **NP** and are such that any polynomial-time algorithm for them can be transformed (in polynomial-time) into a polynomial-time algorithm for every problem in **NP**. Such problems are called **NP-complete**. The problem of trying to find a proper m-coloring of the vertices of a graph, for any fixed integer m greater than 2, is known to be **NP**-complete [1]. Thus, if we are able to show the existence of a polynomial-time algorithm that finds a proper m-coloring of the vertices of a graph (whenever such a coloring exists, for a fixed integer m greater than 2), we could prove that **P** = **NP**. The present algorithm is, so far as we know, a promising candidate for the task. One of the greatest unresolved problems in mathematics and computer science today is whether **P** = **NP** or **P** $\neq$ **NP** [3].

3. Algorithm

We now present a formal description of the algorithm. This is followed by a small example illustrating the steps of the algorithm. We start with the Cartesian Lemma [15] that allows us to convert the problem of finding a proper m-coloring of the n vertices of a graph to the logically equivalent problem of finding an independent set of size n in the Cartesian product $G \times K_m$.

The Cartesian Lemma. A simple graph G with n vertices is m-colorable if and only if the Cartesian product $G \times K_m$ has an independent set of size n.

Proof. Suppose there is a proper m-coloring of the vertices of G. Define a subset S of vertices of the Cartesian product $G \times K_m$ as follows. A vertex (u, v) of $G \times K_m$ belongs to S if and only if the vertex u of G is assigned the color v with respect to the proper m-coloring. Since each vertex of G is assigned a unique color, $|S| = n$. We shall now show that S is an independent set. Given (u_1, v_1) and (u_2, v_2) in S, suppose there is an edge $\{(u_1, v_1), (u_2, v_2)\}$ in $G \times K_m$. Then, by definition of the Cartesian product, there are two possibilities:

- $u_1 = u_2$ and $\{v_1, v_2\}$ is an edge in K_m. But $u_1 = u_2$ implies $v_1 = v_2$, since each vertex in G is assigned a unique color. But then $\{v_1, v_1\}$ cannot be an edge in K_m since K_m is a simple graph (contradiction).
- $\{u_1, u_2\}$ is an edge in G and $v_1 = v_2$. But this violates the definition of a proper m-coloring of G since adjacent vertices must be assigned different colors (contradiction).

Thus there cannot be an edge between any two vertices in S and S must be an independent set.

Conversely, suppose there is an independent set S of size n in the Cartesian product $G \times K_m$. We shall show that G has a proper m-coloring. If m is greater than or equal to n then G can be trivially m-colored, so assume that m is less than n. Partition the vertices of S into at most m equivalence classes $C_1, C_2,..., C_m$ where a vertex (u, v) in S belongs to the equivalence class C_i if and only if $v = v_i$. Clearly, this gives a well-defined partition of the vertices of S. Now partition the vertices of G into at most m equivalence classes $C'_1, C'_2, ..., C'_m$ where a vertex u of G belongs to the equivalence class C'_i if and only if (u, v_i) belongs to the equivalence class C_i. To show that this gives a well-defined partition of the vertices of G observe that:

- Given a vertex u of G, if u belongs to both C'_i and C'_j then (u, v_i) belongs to C_i and (u, v_j) belongs to C_j. Since K_m is complete, $\{v_i, v_j\}$ is an edge in K_m, so $\{(u, v_i), (u, v_j)\}$ is an edge in the Cartesian product $G \times K_m$. This contradicts the fact that S is an independent set. Thus, the sets $C'_1, C'_2,..., C'_m$ are pairwise disjoint.
- List the elements of S according to the following scheme
  - $(u^1_1, v_1), (u^1_2, v_1), ..., (u^1_{i(1)}, v_1)$
  - $(u^2_1, v_2), (u^2_2, v_2), ..., (u^2_{i(2)}, v_2)$
  - ...
  - $(u^m_1, v_m), (u^m_2, v_m), ..., (u^m_{i(m)}, v_m)$

If some $u^i_j = u^k_l$ in the list, then, since K_m is complete, $\{v_i, v_l\}$ is an edge in K_m, so $\{(u^i_j, v_i), (u^k_l, v_l)\}$ is an edge in the Cartesian product $G \times K_m$. This contradicts the fact that S is an independent set. Thus, all the u^i_j that appear in the list are distinct and, since $|S| = n$, there are n distinct u^i_j. Hence, every vertex of G is contained in some equivalence class C'_i.

Assign color i to vertex u of G if u belongs to the equivalence class C'_i. This gives a proper m-coloring of the vertices of G. $\square$

We now define two procedures for working with independent sets in the Cartesian product $G \times K_m$.

3.1. Procedure. Given an independent set S of the Cartesian product $G \times K_m$, if S has no adjoinable vertices, output S. Else, for each adjoinable vertex (u, v) of S, find the number $\rho(S \cup \{(u, v)\})$ of adjoinable vertices of the independent set $S \cup \{(u, v)\}$. Let $(u, v)_{max}$ denote an adjoinable vertex such that $\rho(S \cup \{(u, v)_{max}\})$ is a maximum and obtain the independent set $S \cup \{(u, v)_{max}\}$. Repeat until the independent set has no adjoinable vertices.

3.2. Procedure. Given a maximal independent set S of the Cartesian product $G \times K_m$, if there is no vertex (u_1, v_1) outside S such that (u_1, v_1) has exactly one neighbor (u_2, v_2) inside S, output S. Else, find a vertex (u_1, v_1) outside S such that (u_1, v_1) has exactly one neighbor (u_2, v_2) inside S. Define $S^{(u_1, v_1), (u_2, v_2)}$ by adjoining (u_1, v_1) to S and removing (u_2, v_2) from S. Perform procedure 3.1 on $S^{(u_1, v_1), (u_2, v_2)}$ and output the resulting independent set.

3.3. Algorithm. Given as input a simple graph G with n vertices, search for a proper m-coloring of the vertices of G. Let $\{u_1, u_2, ..., u_n\}$ denote the vertices of G and let $\{v_1, v_2, ..., v_m\}$ denote the vertices of K_m. We generate maximal independent sets in the Cartesian product $G \times K_m$. At each stage, if the independent set obtained has size at least n, then go to part III.

- **Part I.** For $i = 1, 2, ..., n$ and $j = 1, 2, ..., m$ in turn
  - Initialize the independent set $S_{i,j} = \{(u_i, v_j)\}$.
  - Perform procedure 3.1 on $S_{i,j}$.
  - For $r = 1, 2, ..., n$ perform procedure 3.2 repeated r times.
  - The result is a maximal independent set $S_{i,j}$.
- **Part II.** For each pair of maximal independent sets $S_{i,j}$, $S_{k,l}$ found in part I
  - Initialize the independent set $S_{i,j,k,l} = S_{i,j} \cap S_{k,l}$.
  - Perform procedure 3.1 on $S_{i,j,k,l}$.
  - For $r = 1, 2, ..., n$ perform procedure 3.2 repeated r times.
  - The result is a maximal independent set $S_{i,j,k,l}$.
- **Part III.** If an independent set S of size n has been found at any stage of part I or part II, output S as a proper m-coloring of the vertices of G according to the Cartesian lemma. Else, report that the algorithm could not find any proper m-coloring of the vertices of G.

3.4. Example. We demonstrate the steps of the algorithm with a small example. The input graph is shown below in figure 3.1 with $n = 4$ vertices labeled $V = \{1, 2, 3, 4\}$. The algorithm searches for a proper 3-coloring of the vertices using the set of colors $\{1, 2, 3\}$ represented by green, red and blue respectively.

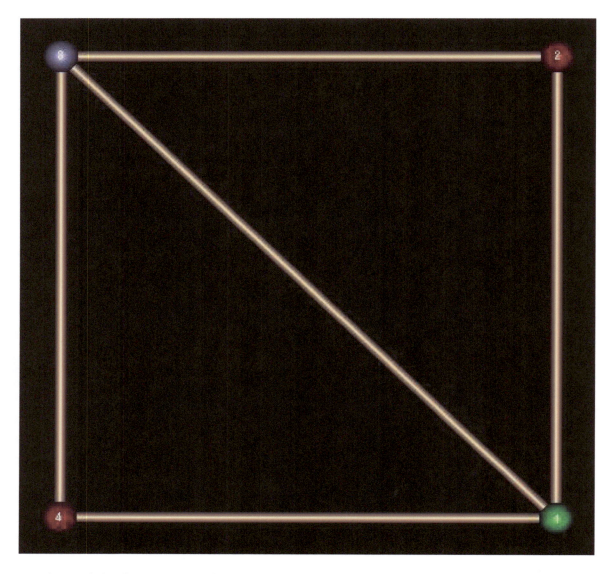

Figure 3.1. *The input graph G with q proper 3-coloring {(1, 1), (2, 2), (3, 3), (4, 2)} of its vertices found by the algorithm*

The algorithm first constructs the Cartesian product $G \times K_3$ shown below in figure 3.2 with 12 vertices {(1,1), (1,2), (1,3), (2,1), (2,2), (2,3), (3,1), (3,2), (3,3), (4,1), (4,2), (4,3)}. We construe the vertices {1, 2, 3} of the second component K_3 as the colors green, red and blue respectively.

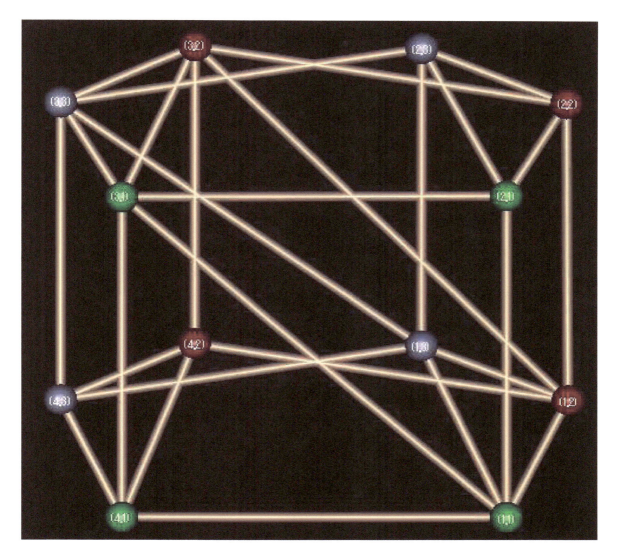

Figure 3.2. *The Cartesian product G×K₃ with an independent set*
{(1, 1), (2, 2), (3, 3), (4, 2)} of size 4 found by the algorithm

The algorithm now searches for an independent set of size 4 in the Cartesian product $G \times K_3$. Part I for $i = 1$ and $j = 1$ initializes the independent set as

$$S_{1,1} = \{(1, 1)\}.$$

We now perform procedure 3.1. Here are the results in tabular form:

Independent Set $S_{1,1} = \{(1, 1)\}$. Size: 1.

Adjoinable vertex (u, v) of $S_{1,1}$	Adjoinable vertices of $S_{1,1} \cup \{(u, v)\}$	$\rho(S_{1,1} \cup \{(u, v)\})$
(2, 2)	(3, 3), (4, 2), (4, 3)	3
(2, 3)	(3, 2), (4, 2), (4, 3)	3
(3, 2)	(2, 3), (4, 3)	2
(3, 3)	(2, 2), (4, 2)	2
(4, 2)	(2, 2), (2, 3), (3, 3)	3
(4, 3)	(2, 2), (2, 3), (3, 2)	3

Maximum $\rho(S_{1,1} \cup \{(u, v)\}) = 3$ for $(u, v) = (2, 2)$. Adjoin vertex $(2, 2)$ to $S_{1,1}$.

Independent Set $S_{1,1} = \{(1, 1), (2, 2)\}$. Size: 2.

Adjoinable vertex (u, v) of $S_{1,1}$	Adjoinable vertices of $S_{1,1} \cup \{(u, v)\}$	$\rho(S_{1,1} \cup \{(u, v)\})$
(3, 3)	(4, 2)	1
(4, 2)	(3, 3)	1
(4, 3)	None	0

Maximum $\rho(S_{1,1} \cup \{(u, v)\}) = 1$ for $(u, v) = (3, 3)$. Adjoin vertex $(3, 3)$ to $S_{1,1}$.

Independent Set $S_{1,1} = \{(1, 1), (2, 2), (3, 3)\}$. Size: 3.

Adjoinable vertex (u, v) of $S_{1,1}$	Adjoinable vertices of $S_{1,1} \cup \{(u, v)\}$	$\rho(S_{1,1} \cup \{(u, v)\})$
(4, 2)	None	0

Maximum $\rho(S_{1,1} \cup \{(u, v)\}) = 0$ for $(u, v) = (4, 2)$. Adjoin vertex $(4, 2)$ to $S_{1,1}$.

We obtain a maximal independent set

$$S_{1,1} = \{(1, 1), (2, 2), (3, 3), (4, 2)\}$$

of the required size $n = 4$. Now part III outputs $S_{1,1}$ as the requested proper 3-coloring of the input graph G and the algorithm terminates. Note that we interpret the result as follows: vertex 1 is colored with color 1 (green), vertex 2 is colored with color 2 (red), vertex 3 is colored with color 3 (blue) and vertex 4 is colored with color 2 (red).

4. Complexity

We shall now show that the algorithm terminates in polynomial-time while searching for a proper m-coloring for a graph with n vertices, by specifying a polynomial of $N = nm$ that is an upper bound on the total number of computational steps performed by the algorithm. Note that we consider

- checking whether a given pair of vertices is connected by an edge in G, and
- comparing whether a given integer is less than another given integer

to be *elementary computational steps*.

4.1. Proposition. Given a simple graph G with n vertices and an independent set S of $G{\times}K_m$, procedure 3.1 takes at most $(nm)^5$ steps.

Proof. Checking whether a particular vertex is adjoinable takes at most $(nm)^2$ steps, since the vertex has less than nm neighbors and for each neighbor it takes less than nm steps to check whether it is outside the independent set. For a particular independent set, finding the number ρ of adjoinable vertices takes at most $(nm)^3 = (nm)(nm)^2$ steps, since for each of the at most nm vertices outside the independent set we must check whether it is adjoinable or not. For a particular independent set, finding a vertex for which ρ is maximum then takes at most $(nm)^4 = (nm)(nm)^3$ steps, since there are at most nm vertices outside. Procedure 3.1 terminates when at most nm vertices are adjoined, so it takes a total of at most $(nm)^5 = (nm)(nm)^4$ steps. $\square$

4.2. Proposition. Given a simple graph G with n vertices and a maximal independent set S of $G{\times}K_m$, procedure 3.2 takes at most $(nm)^5 + (nm)^2 + 1$ steps.

Proof. To find a vertex (u_1, v_1) outside S that has exactly one neighbor (u_2, v_2) inside S takes at most $(nm)^2$ steps, since there are less than nm vertices outside S and we must find out if at least one of the less than nm neighbors of any such vertex are inside S. If such a vertex (u_1, v_1) has been found, it takes one step to exchange (u_1, v_1) and (u_2, v_2). Thereafter, by proposition 4.1, it takes at most $(nm)^5$ steps to perform procedure 3.1 on the resulting independent set. Thus, procedure 3.2 takes at most $(nm)^2 + 1 + (nm)^5$ steps. $\square$

4.3. Proposition. Given a simple graph G with n vertices and m colors, part I of the algorithm takes at most $(nm)^7 + (nm)^6 + (nm)^4 + (nm)^2$ steps.

Proof. At each turn, procedure 3.1 takes at most $(nm)^5$ steps by proposition 4.1. Then procedure 3.2 is performed at most nm times which, by proposition 4.2, takes at most $nm((nm)^5 + (nm)^2 + 1) = (nm)^6 + (nm)^3 + nm$ steps. So, at each turn, at most $(nm)^5 + (nm)^6 + (nm)^3 + nm$ steps are executed. There are nm turns for $i = 1, 2, ..., n$, and $j = 1, 2, ..., m$, so part I performs a total of at most $nm((nm)^5 + (nm)^6 + (nm)^3 + nm) = (nm)^6 + (nm)^7 + (nm)^4 + (nm)^2$ steps. $\square$

4.4. Proposition. Given a simple graph G with n vertices and m colors, the algorithm takes less than $(nm)^8+2(nm)^7+(nm)^6+(nm)^5+(nm)^4+(nm)^3+(nm)^2$ steps to terminate.

Proof. There are less than $(nm)^2$ distinct pairs of maximal independent sets found by part I, that are treated in turn. Similar to the proof of proposition 4.3, part II takes less than $(nm)^2((nm)^5+(nm)^6+(nm)^3+nm) = (nm)^7+(nm)^8+(nm)^5+(nm)^3$. Hence, part I and part II together take less than a grand total of
$((nm)^7+(nm)^6+(nm)^4+(nm)^2)+((nm)^8+(nm)^7+(nm)^5+(nm)^3) = (nm)^8+2(nm)^7+(nm)^6+(nm)^5+(nm)^4+(nm)^3+(nm)^2$ steps to terminate. $\square$

4.5. Remark. These are pessimistic upper bounds for the worst possible cases. The actual number of steps taken by the algorithm will depend on both n and m and, for all the known cases when a proper m-coloring of the vertices exists, the algorithm terminates much faster. In all of the examples in section 7, one or two steps of part I already find a proper m-coloring of the vertices of the graph.

5. Sufficiency

Given m colors, the algorithm may be applied to any simple graph G with n vertices. The algorithm will always terminate in polynomial-time, finding many maximal independent sets in the Cartesian product $G \times K_m$. The propositions below establish sufficient conditions on the number of colors m and the input graph G, which guarantee that the algorithm will find maximal independent sets of size at least n in the Cartesian product $G \times K_m$ and a proper m-coloring of the vertices of G. Specifically, we prove that every graph with n vertices and maximum vertex degree Δ must have chromatic number $\chi(G)$ less than or equal to $\Delta+1$ and that the algorithm will always find a proper m-coloring of the vertices of G with m less than or equal to $\Delta+1$. Furthermore, we prove that this condition is the best possible in terms of n and Δ by explicitly constructing graphs for which the chromatic number is exactly $\Delta+1$. In the special case when G is a connected simple graph and is neither an odd cycle nor a complete graph, we show that the algorithm will always find a proper m-coloring of the vertices of G with m less than or equal to Δ. In the process, we obtain a new constructive proof of Brooks' famous theorem of 1941. The following proofs use two fundamental axioms: Euclid's Division Lemma [5] and the Pigeonhole Principle [6].

Euclid's Division Lemma. Given a positive integer m and any integer n, there exist unique integers q and r with $0 \le r < m$ such that $n = qm+r$.

Pigeonhole Principle. If l letters are distributed into p pigeonholes, then some pigeonhole receives at least $\lceil l/p \rceil$ letters and some pigeonhole receives at most $\lfloor l/p \rfloor$ letters.

5.1. Proposition. Given a simple graph G with n vertices, m colors and an initial independent set S of $G \times K_m$. At each stage of procedure 3.1, if there are l vertices outside S and the maximum degree among the vertices inside S is less than $\lceil l/(nm-l) \rceil$, then procedure 3.1 produces a strictly larger independent set.

Proof. By contradiction. Suppose the independent set S is maximal. Then there are no adjoinable vertices and every vertex outside S must have a neighbor inside S. Thus there are at least l edges (letters) with one end vertex outside S and the other end vertex inside S, there being exactly $p = nm-l$ vertices inside S (pigeonholes). By the pigeonhole principle, some vertex inside S must receive at least $\lceil l/p \rceil$ edges contradicting the hypothesis that the maximum degree among the vertices inside S is less than $\lceil l/p \rceil$. $\square$

5.2. Proposition. Given a simple graph G with n vertices, m colors and an independent set S of $G \times K_m$, procedure 3.1 always produces a maximal independent set of $G \times K_m$.

Proof. Procedure 3.1 terminates only when there are no adjoinable vertices. By definition, the resulting independent set must be maximal. $\square$

5.3. Proposition. Given a simple graph G with n vertices, m colors and an initial maximal independent set S of $G \times K_m$. If there are t vertices outside the maximal independent set S and the maximum degree among the vertices inside S is less than $\lceil 2t/(nm-t) \rceil$, then there exists a vertex (u_1, v_1) outside S such that (u_1, v_1) has exactly one neighbor (u_2, v_2) inside S and procedure 3.2 produces a maximal independent set different from S and of size greater than or equal to the size of S.

Proof. By contradiction. Note that since S is maximal, there are no adjoinable vertices and every vertex outside S has at least one neighbor inside S. Suppose every vertex outside S has more than one neighbor inside S. Then there are at least $l = 2t$ edges (letters) with one end vertex outside S and the other end vertex inside S, there being exactly $p = nm-t$ vertices inside S (pigeonholes). By the pigeonhole principle, some vertex inside S must receive at least $\lceil l/p \rceil$ edges contradicting the hypothesis that the maximum degree among the vertices inside S is less than $\lceil l/p \rceil$. Thus, there exists a vertex (u_1, v_1) outside S such that (u_1, v_1) has exactly one neighbor (u_2, v_2) inside S. Now since procedure 3.2 exchanges (u_1, v_1) and (u_2, v_2), an independent set different from S but of the same size as S is created. Note that in the process some vertices outside the independent set might have become adjoinable. Then, procedure 3.2 applies procedure 3.1 that produces a maximal independent set different from S and of size greater than or equal to the size of S. $\square$

5.4. Proposition. Given a simple graph G with n vertices and m colors. If G has maximum vertex degree Δ, then the algorithm always finds a maximal independent set in $G \times K_m$ of size at least $\lceil nm/(\Delta+m) \rceil$.

Proof. Note that the maximum vertex degree of the Cartesian graph $G \times K_m$ is $\Delta+m-1$. Consider any one turn of part I in the algorithm. After t vertices have been adjoined from a total of nm, there are $l = nm-t$ vertices outside the independent set S and the maximum degree among the vertices inside S is certainly less than or equal to $\Delta+m-1$. By proposition 5.1, if $\Delta+m-1$ is less than $\lceil l/(nm-l) \rceil = \lceil (nm-t)/(nm-(nm-t)) \rceil = \lceil (nm-t)/t \rceil = \lceil (nm/t)-1 \rceil$, then a strictly larger independent set is produced by adjoining a vertex. Hence, as long as t is less than $\lceil nm/(\Delta+m-1+1) \rceil = \lceil nm/(\Delta+m) \rceil$, a vertex can still be adjoined and procedure 1 continues. Thus, at least $\lceil nm/(\Delta+m) \rceil$ vertices are adjoined, producing an independent set of size at least $\lceil nm/(\Delta+m) \rceil$. By propositions 5.1, 5.2 and 5.3, all of the independent sets produced by the algorithm are maximal and of size at least $\lceil nm/(\Delta+m) \rceil$. □

5.5. Proposition. Let G be a simple graph with n vertices and maximal vertex degree Δ. Given m colors where m is greater than or equal to $\Delta+1$, the algorithm always finds a proper m-coloring of the vertices of G.

Proof. We shall show that the size of any maximal independent set S found by the algorithm in the cartesian graph $G \times K_m$ is at least n, by contradiction. Suppose the independent set $S = \{(u_1, v_1), (u_2, v_2), ..., (u_k, v_k)\}$ is maximal and k is less than n. Note that $u_1, u_2, ..., u_k$ must be k distinct vertices of G since $u_i = u_j$ implies that there is an edge between (u_i, v_i) and (u_j, v_j) in $G \times K_m$ since K_m is complete. Let u be a vertex of G different from $u_1, u_2, ..., u_k$. Then, for each vertex v of K_m, the vertex (u, v) of $G \times K_m$ is outside S and must have a nieghbor in S since S is a maximal independent set. The only way the vertex (u, v) can have a neighbor (u_i, v_i) in S is if $v = v_i$ and u is a neighbor of u_i in G. Thus the degree of the vertex u is greater than or equal to m in G. This contradicts the hypothesis that m is greater than or equal to $\Delta+1$. □

5.6. Corollary. For any simple graph G with maximal vertex degree Δ, the chromatic number $\chi(G)$ is less than or equal to $\Delta+1$.

Proof. By proposition 5.5, the algorithm always finds a proper m-coloring of the vertices of G for m equal to $\Delta+1$. □

5.7. Proposition. Given any positive integers n and Δ such that $0 < \Delta < n$, there exists a graph G with maximum vertex degree Δ and chromatic number $\chi(G) = \Delta+1$. For any such graph the algorithm always finds a proper m-coloring of the vertices of G for m equal to $\Delta+1$.

Proof. Let $n = q(\Delta+1)+r$ with $0 \leq r < \Delta+1$ by Euclid's division lemma. There are two cases.

- *Case 1.* Suppose $r = 0$. Define G to be the graph consisting of q disjoint cliques $Q_1, ..., Q_q$ with $\Delta+1$ vertices each. Then G is a graph with maximum vertex degree Δ. Each of the disjoint cliques has a proper m-coloring with $m = \Delta+1$ colors and this is the minimum value of m for which the clique has a proper m-coloring, since each vertex of the clique must be assigned a different color. Proper m-coloring of all the q disjoint cliques gives a proper m-coloring of G and this is the minimum value of m for which G has a proper m-coloring. Thus, the chromatic number $\chi(G) = \Delta+1$. By proposition 5.5, the algorithm finds a proper m-coloring of the vertices of G with $m = \Delta+1$ colors.

- *Case* 2. Suppose r is positive. Define G to be the graph consisting of q disjoint cliques $Q_1, ...,Q_q$ with $\Delta+1$ vertices each and a disjoint clique R with r vertices. Then G is a graph with maximum vertex degree Δ. Each of the disjoint cliques Q_i has a proper m-coloring with $m = \Delta+1$ colors and this is the minimum value of m for which the clique Q_i has a proper m-coloring, since each vertex of the clique must be assigned a different color. The clique R certainly has a proper m-coloring where not all of the m colors are used, since $r < \Delta+1$. Proper m-coloring of the disjoint cliques $Q_1, ...,Q_q$ and the disjoint clique R gives a proper m-coloring of G and this is the minimum value of m for which G has a proper m-coloring. Thus, the chromatic number $\chi(G) = \Delta+1$. By proposition 5.5, the algorithm finds a proper m-coloring of the vertices of G with $m = \Delta+1$ colors. $\square$

5.8. Proposition. Let G be a simple graph with n vertices and maximal vertex degree Δ. If G is a connected and is neither an odd cycle nor a complete graph, then the algorithm finds a proper m-coloring of the vertices of G for some m less than or equal to Δ.

Proof. The proposition is trivial if n is less than 3, so assume that n is at least 3. Let $m = \Delta$. First suppose that G is a simple path or an even cycle. Then $m = \Delta = 2$ and the first turn of part I will find a maximal independent set $S = \{(u_1, 1), (u_2, 2), (u_3, 1), (u_4, 2), ..., (u_{n-1}, 1), (u_n, 2)\}$ with alternating colors 1 and 2 such that the simple path or even cycle $u_1, u_2, u_3, u_4, ..., u_{n-1}, u_n$ consists of all the vertices of G. Thus, if G is a simple path or an even cycle then the algorithm finds a proper 2-coloring of G. Since G cannot be an odd cycle by hypothesis, from now on let us assume that G is neither a simple path nor a cycle. Since G is not complete, there exist three vertices u', u'', u''' such that $\{u', u''\}$, $\{u'', u'''\}$ are edges of G and $\{u', u'''\}$ is not an edge of G. Let $u_1 = u'$ and $v_1 = 1$. Let $S = \{(u_1, v_1), (u_2, v_2), ..., (u_k, v_k)\}$ be the maximal independent set of $G \times K_m$ generated by the turn of part I starting with (u_1, v_1) and suppose k is less than n. Note that $u_1, u_2, ..., u_k$ must be k distinct vertices of G since $u_i = u_j$ implies that there is an edge between (u_i, v_i) and (u_j, v_j) in $G \times K_m$, since K_m is complete.

- **(i)** Suppose u is vertex of G distinct from $u_1, u_2, ..., u_k$. Then $(u, 1), (u, 2), ..., (u, m)$ are all outside S. Since S is a maximal independent set, there must be m edges $\{(u, 1), (u_{i(1)}, 1)\}$, $\{(u, 2), (u_{i(2)}, 2)\}$, ..., $\{(u, m), (u_{i(m)}, m)\}$ in $G \times K_m$. Thus u has m neighbors $u_{i(1)}, u_{i(2)}, ..., u_{i(m)}$ in G. Since $m = \Delta$ by hypothesis, u has maximum degree Δ in G and $u_{i(1)}, u_{i(2)}, ..., u_{i(m)}$ are all the neighbors of u in G. This implies that each (u, j) has exactly one neighbor $(u_{i(j)}, j)$ in S, for $j = 1, 2, ..., m$. Thus, for each $j = 1, 2, ..., m$, we can form the maximal independent set $S^{(u, j),(u_{i(j)}, j)}$ by adjoining (u, j) to S, removing $(u_{i(j)}, j)$ from S and performing procedure 3.1.
- **(ii)** Suppose there are more than one vertices $u_{k+1}, u_{k+2}, ...$ of G distinct from $u_1, u_2, ..., u_k$. Since G is connected, there is a path from u_{k+1} to u_{k+2} in G, say $u_{k+1} = w_1, w_2, ..., w_l = u_{k+2}$. Starting from w_1 in the path, let $w_{l'} = u_{k'+2}$ be the first vertex that is distinct from $u_1, u_2, ..., u_k, u_{k+1}$. Then $(w_2, v_{j(2)}), ..., (w_{l'-1}, v_{j(l'-1)})$ all belong to

S for some vertices $v_{j(2)}$, ..., $v_{j(l'-1)}$ of K_m. By (i), we can generate a sequence of maximal independent sets as follows:

- $S_1 = S^{(w_1, v_{j(1)}),(w_2, v_{j(2)})}$, maximal independent set obtained by adjoining $(w_1, v_{j(1)})$ to S, removing $(w_2, v_{j(2)})$ from S and performing procedure 3.1.

- $S_2 = S_1^{(w_2, v_{j(2)}),(w_3, v_{j(3)})}$, maximal independent set obtained by adjoining $(w_2, v_{j(2)})$ to S_1, removing $(w_3, v_{j(3)})$ from S_1 and performing procedure 3.1.

- ...

- $S_{l'-1} = S_{l'-2}^{(w_{l'-1}, v_{j(l'-1)}),(w_{l'}, v_{j(l')})}$, maximal independent set obtained by adjoining $(w_{l'-1}, v_{j(l'-1)})$ to $S_{l'-2}$, removing $(w_{l'}, v_{j(l')})$ from $S_{l'-2}$ and performing procedure 3.1.

Note that in this process every element of S that was removed was replaced back and $(w_1, v_{j(1)}) = (u_{k+1}, v_{j(1)})$ (and possibly others) were adjoined. This means that $S_{l'-1}$ is a maximal independent set that properly contains the maximal independent set S, a contradiction. Hence, there can be at most one vertex u_{k+1} of G distinct from $u_1, u_2, ..., u_k$.

- **(iii)** By (ii) and the assumption that k is less than n, the maximal independent set S = $\{(u_1, v_1), (u_2, v_2), ..., (u_{n-1}, v_{n-1})\}$ and there is exactly one vertex u_n of G distinct from $u_1, u_2, ..., u_{n-1}$.

- **(iv)** We shall derive a contradiction to (iii) by following through the construction of the maximal independent set S. Consider the turn of part I starting with S = $\{(u', 1)\}$. Now procedure 3.1 is performed. The adjoinable vertices (u, v) of S are vertices of $G \times K_m$ of the following two types:

  - **Type 1.** (u is distinct from u' in G) and ($\{u, u'\}$ is not an edge in G) and ($v = 1$ in K_m)

    or

  - **Type 2.** (u is distinct from u' in G) and (v is distinct from 1 in K_m).

Now suppose a vertex (u, v) is adjoined and S = $\{(u', 1), (u, v)\}$. There are two cases:

  - **Case 1.** If (u, v) is a vertex of type 1, then the adjoinable vertices (x, y) of S are vertices of $G \times K_m$ of the following two types:
    - **Type 1(a).** (x, u', u are distinct in G) and ($\{x, u'\}$ is not an edge in G) and ($\{x, u\}$ is not an edge in G) and ($y = 1$ in K_m)

      or
    - **Type 1(b).** (x, u', u are distinct in G) and (y is distinct from 1 in K_m).

  - **Case 2.** If (u, v) is a vertex of type 2, then the adjoinable vertices (x, y) of S are vertices of $G \times K_m$ of the following three types:
    - **Type 2(a).** (x, u', u are distinct in G) and ($\{x, u'\}$ is not an edge in G) and ($y = 1$ in K_m)

      or

- **Type 2(b).** (x, u', u are distinct in G) and ($\{x, u\}$ is not an edge in G) and ($y = v$ in K_m)

  or

- **Type 2(c).** (x, u', u are distinct in G) and (y, 1, v are distinct in K_m).

We now show that there are at least as many adjoinable vertices in case 1 as there are in case 2, as follows:

- In case 2, if (x, y) is adjoinable of type 2(b), then the same (x, y) is adjoinable of type 1(b) in case 1.
- In case 2, if (x, y) is adjoinable of type 2(c), then the same (x, y) is adjoinable of type 1(b) in case 1.
- In case 2, suppose (x, y) is adjoinable of type 2(a). Now since G is neither a simple path nor a cycle, the maximum degree $\Delta = m$ is at least 3. Hence there exists a vertex v' distinct from 1 and v in K_m. Then (x, v') is adjoinable of type 1(b) in case 1, ensuring that we have not counted the same (x, v') more than once.

We now show that there is at least one more adjoinable vertex in case 1 compared to case 2. Let $u = u'''$. Then for $x = u''$ in case 2, (u'', y) must be adjoinable of type 2(c) because $\{u', u''\}$ and $\{u'', u'''\}$ are edges of G. There are only $m-2$ choices for y, since y, 1, v are distinct in K_m by definition of type 2(c). All these (u'', y) are also adjoinable of type 1(b) in case 1. However, in case 1, there is an extra choice available, namely $y = v$. Thus, the number ρ of adjoinable vertices of $S = \{(u', 1), (u, v)\}$ is strictly greater in case 1 where (u, v) is of type 1 and procedure 3.1 adjoins (u, v) of type 1. Continuing in this way, comparing vertices of $G \times K_m$ of type 1 and type 2 pairwise and applying procedure 3.1, we must arrive at an independent set $S = \{ (u_1, v_1) = (u', 1), (u_2, 1), ..., (u_t, 1)\}$ where u_t is such that for some x, $\{u', x\}$, $\{x, u_t\}$ are edges of G and $\{u', u_t\}$ is not an edge of G. By hypothesis such vertices exist and we may assume without loss of generality that $u_t = u'''$ and $x = u''$. Continuing to apply procedure 3.1 we finally arrive at a maximal independent set $S = \{ (u_1, v_1) = (u', 1), (u_2, v_2), ..., (u_t, 1) = (u''', 1), ..., (u_{n-1}, v_{n-1})\}$ and there is exactly one vertex u_n of G distinct from $u_1, u_2, ..., u_{n-1}$. Now there are two cases:

- **Case 1'.** $u_n = u''$. Since $\Delta = m$ and u'' has two neighbors u, u''' both of color 1, at most $m-2$ other colors are adjacent to u''. Including 1, at most $m-1$ colors are adjacent to u'' and there is always a color v'' left for u''. But then we can adjoin (u_n, v_n) = (u'', v'') to the maximal independent set S, a contradiction.
- **Case 2'.** u_n and u'' are distinct. Then u'' is one of $u_1, u_2, ..., u_{n-1}$. Since G is connected, there is a path from u_n to u'', say $u_n = w_1, w_2, ..., w_l = u''$. Then ($w_2$, $v_{j(2)}$), ..., (w_{l-1}, $v_{j(l-1)}$) all belong to S for some vertices $v_{j(2)}, ..., v_{j(l-1)}$ of K_m. By (i), we can generate a sequence of maximal independent sets as follows:

- $S_1 = S^{(w_1, v_{j(1)}),(w_2, v_{j(2)})}$, maximal independent set obtained by adjoining $(w_1, v_{j(1)})$ to S, removing $(w_2, v_{j(2)})$ from S and performing procedure 3.1.
- $S_2 = S_1^{(w_2, v_{j(2)}),(w_3, v_{j(3)})}$, maximal independent set obtained by adjoining $(w_2, v_{j(2)})$ to S_1, removing $(w_3, v_{j(3)})$ from S_1 and performing procedure 3.1.
- ...
- $S_{l-1} = S_{l-2}^{(w_{l-1}, v_{j(l-1)}),(w_l, v_{j(l)})}$, maximal independent set obtained by adjoining $(w_{l-1}, v_{j(l-1)})$ to S_{l-2}, removing $(w_l, v_{j(l)})$ from S_{l-2} and performing procedure 3.1.

Note that in the process

- $(u_n, v_{j(1)}) = (w_1, v_{j(1)})$ was adjoined and never removed.
- $(u'', v_{j(l)}) = (w_l, v_{j(l)})$ was removed and never adjoined.
- Every other element was removed and replaced back.

o Thus, $S_{l-1} = \{(u'_1, v'_1), (u'_2, v'_2), ..., (u'_{n-1}, v'_{n-1})\}$ is a maximal independent set where $u'_1, u'_2, ..., u'_{n-1}$ are distinct vertices of G, u'' is distinct from $u'_1, u'_2, ..., u'_{n-1}$ and for some i, j we have $(u'_i, v'_i) = (u', 1)$, $(u'_j, v'_j) = (u''', 1)$. Now, exactly as in case 1', we obtain a contradiction.

By (i), (ii), (iii) and (iv), we must have $k = n$ and the maximal independent set $S = \{(u_1, v_1), (u_2, v_2), ..., (u_n, v_n)\}$. Thus, the algorithm finds a proper m-coloring of the vertices of G. $\square$

5.9. Corollary [Brooks' Theorem, 1941]. Let G be a simple graph with n vertices and maximal vertex degree Δ. If G is a connected and is neither an odd cycle nor a complete graph, then the chromatic number $\chi(G)$ is less than or equal to Δ.

Proof. By proposition 5.8, the algorithm finds a proper m-coloring of G for some m less than or equal to Δ. $\square$

5.10. Question. For all known examples of graphs, the algorithm finds a proper m-coloring of the vertices of the graph G for m equal to the chromatic number $\chi(G)$. In view of the importance of the **P** versus **NP** question [3], we ask: *does there exist a graph G for which this algorithm cannot find a proper m-coloring of the vertices of G with m equal to the chromatic number $\chi(G)$?*

6. Implementation

We demonstrate the algorithm with a C++ program following the style of **[7]**. The demonstration program package **[download]** contains a detailed help file and section 7 gives several examples of input/output files for the program.

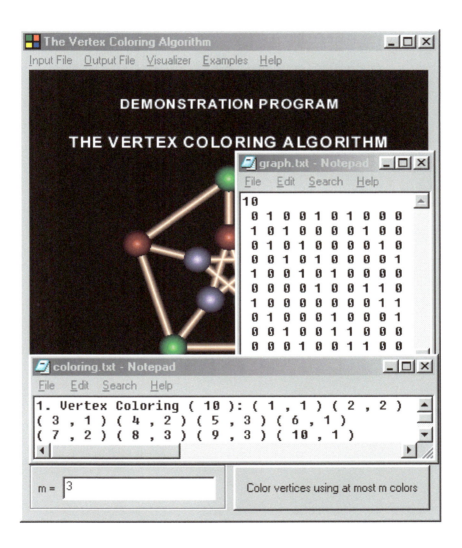

Figure 6.1. *Demonstration program for Microsoft Windows* **[download]**

```cpp
vertex_coloring.cpp
#include <iostream>
#include <fstream>
#include <string>
#include <vector>
using namespace std;

bool removable(vector<int> neighbor, vector<int> cover);
int max_removable(vector<vector<int> > neighbors, vector<int> cover);
vector<int> procedure_1(vector<vector<int> > neighbors, vector<int>
cover);
vector<int> procedure_2(vector<vector<int> > neighbors, vector<int>
cover, int k);
int cover_size(vector<int> cover);
ifstream infile ("graph.txt");
ofstream outfile ("coloring.txt");

int main()
{
 //Read Graph
 cout<<"Vertex Coloring Algorithm."<<endl;
 int C, N, n, i, j, k, K, p, q, r, s, min, edge, counter=0;
 infile>>N;
 vector< vector<int> > Graph;
 for(i=0; i<N; i++)
 {
  vector<int> row;
  for(j=0; j<N; j++)
  {
   infile>>edge;
   row.push_back(edge);
  }
  Graph.push_back(row);
 }
 //COLORING to INDEPENDENT SET conversion
 cout<<"Graph has N = "<<N<<" vertices."<<endl;
 cout<<"Find a vertex coloring using at most C colors. Enter C = ";
 cin>>C;
  //Complete garph on C verteices
  vector<vector<int> > KC;
  vector<int> row1;
  for(int i=0; i<C; i++) row1.push_back(1);
  for(int i=0; i<C; i++) KC.push_back(row1);
  for(int i=0; i<C; i++) KC[i][i]=0;
  //Cartesian product of Graph and KC
  vector<vector<int> > graph;
  vector<int> rowind;
  for(int i=0; i<C*N; i++) rowind.push_back(0);
  for(int i=0; i<C*N; i++) graph.push_back(rowind);
  for(int i=0; i<C*N; i++)
  for(int j=0; j<C*N; j++)
  {
   int i_G=i/C, i_KC=i%C, j_G=j/C, j_KC=j%C;
   if((i_G==j_G) && (KC[i_KC][j_KC]==1)) graph[i][j]=1;
   if((Graph[i_G][j_G]==1) && (i_KC==j_KC)) graph[i][j]=1;
  }
```

```cpp
    //Assign parameters for finding independent sets in the graph
    n=N*C; K=n/C; k=n-K;
    //Find Neighbors
    vector<vector<int> > neighbors;
    for(i=0; i<graph.size(); i++)
    {
     vector<int> neighbor;
     for(j=0; j<graph[i].size(); j++)
     if(graph[i][j]==1) neighbor.push_back(j);
     neighbors.push_back(neighbor);
    }

    //Find Independent Sets
    bool found=false;
    cout<<"Finding Vertex Colorings..."<<endl;
    min=n+1;
    vector<vector<int> > covers;
    vector<int> allcover;
    for(i=0; i<graph.size(); i++)
    allcover.push_back(1);
    for(i=0; i<allcover.size(); i++)
    {
     if(found) break;
     counter++; cout<<counter<<". ";  outfile<<counter<<". ";
     vector<int> cover=allcover;
     cover[i]=0;
     cover=procedure_1(neighbors,cover);
     s=cover_size(cover);
     if(s<min) min=s;
     if(s<=k)
     {
      outfile<<"Vertex Coloring ("<<n-s<<"): ";
      for(j=0; j<cover.size(); j++) if(cover[j]==0)
    outfile<<" ("<<j/C+1<<","<<j%C+1<<") ";
      outfile<<endl;
      cout<<"Vertex Coloring Size: "<<n-s<<endl;
      covers.push_back(cover);
      found=true;
      break;
     }
     for(j=0; j<n-k; j++)
     cover=procedure_2(neighbors,cover,j);
     s=cover_size(cover);
     if(s<min) min=s;
     outfile<<"Vertex Coloring ("<<n-s<<"): ";
     for(j=0; j<cover.size(); j++) if(cover[j]==0)
    outfile<<" ("<<j/C+1<<","<<j%C+1<<") ";
     outfile<<endl;
     cout<<"Vertex Coloring Size: "<<n-s<<endl;
     covers.push_back(cover);
     if(s<=k){ found=true; break; }
    }
    //Pairwise Intersections
    for(p=0; p<covers.size(); p++)
    {
     if(found) break;
```

```cpp
   for(q=p+1; q<covers.size(); q++)
   {
    if(found) break;
    counter++; cout<<counter<<". ";  outfile<<counter<<". ";
    vector<int> cover=allcover;
    for(r=0; r<cover.size(); r++)
    if(covers[p][r]==0 && covers[q][r]==0) cover[r]=0;
    cover=procedure_1(neighbors,cover);
    s=cover_size(cover);
    if(s<min) min=s;
    if(s<=k)
    {
     outfile<<"Vertex Coloring ("<<n-s<<"): ";
     for(j=0; j<cover.size(); j++) if(cover[j]==0)
outfile<<" ("<<j/C+1<<","<<j%C+1<<") ";
     outfile<<endl;
     cout<<"Vertex Coloring Size: "<<n-s<<endl;
     found=true;
     break;
    }
    for(j=0; j<k; j++)
    cover=procedure_2(neighbors,cover,j);
    s=cover_size(cover);
    if(s<min) min=s;
    outfile<<"Vertex Coloring ("<<n-s<<"): ";
    for(j=0; j<cover.size(); j++) if(cover[j]==0)
outfile<<" ("<<j/C+1<<","<<j%C+1<<") ";
    outfile<<endl;
    cout<<"Vertex Coloring Size: "<<n-s<<endl;
    if(s<=k){ found=true; break; }
    }
  }
 if(found) cout<<"Found  complete Vertex Coloring using at most "<<C<<"
colors."<<endl;
 else cout<<"Could not find complete Vertex Coloring using at most
"<<C<<" colors."<<endl
 <<"Maximum partial Vertex Coloring found for "<<n-min<<"
vertices."<<endl;
 cout<<"See coloring.txt for results."<<endl;
 system("PAUSE");
 return 0;
}


bool removable(vector<int> neighbor, vector<int> cover)
{
 bool check=true;
 for(int i=0; i<neighbor.size(); i++)
 if(cover[neighbor[i]]==0)
 {
  check=false;
  break;
 }
 return check;
}
```

```
int max_removable(vector<vector<int> > neighbors, vector<int> cover)
{
 int r=-1, max=-1;
 for(int i=0; i<cover.size(); i++)
 {
  if(cover[i]==1 && removable(neighbors[i],cover)==true)
  {
   vector<int> temp_cover=cover;
   temp_cover[i]=0;
   int sum=0;
   for(int j=0; j<temp_cover.size(); j++)
   if(temp_cover[j]==1 && removable(neighbors[j], temp_cover)==true)
   sum++;
   if(sum>max)
   {
    max=sum;
    r=i;
   }
  }
 }
 return r;
}


vector<int> procedure_1(vector<vector<int> > neighbors, vector<int>
cover)
{
 vector<int> temp_cover=cover;
 int r=0;
 while(r!=-1)
 {
  r= max_removable(neighbors,temp_cover);
  if(r!=-1) temp_cover[r]=0;
 }
 return temp_cover;
}


vector<int> procedure_2(vector<vector<int> > neighbors, vector<int>
cover, int k)
{
 int count=0;
 vector<int> temp_cover=cover;
 int i=0;
 for(int i=0; i<temp_cover.size(); i++)
 {
  if(temp_cover[i]==1)
  {
   int sum=0, index;
   for(int j=0; j<neighbors[i].size(); j++)
   if(temp_cover[neighbors[i][j]]==0) {index=j; sum++;}
   if(sum==1 && cover[neighbors[i][index]]==0)
   {
    temp_cover[neighbors[i][index]]=1;
    temp_cover[i]=0;
    temp_cover=procedure_1(neighbors,temp_cover);
    count++;
   }
```

```
    if(count>k) break;
  }
 }
 return temp_cover;
}

int cover_size(vector<int> cover)
{
 int count=0;
 for(int i=0; i<cover.size(); i++)
 if(cover[i]==1) count++;
 return count;
}
```

Figure 6.2. C++ *program for the vertex coloring algorithm* **[download]**

7. Examples

We demonstrate the algorithm by running the program on several famous graphs, including a proper four-coloring of the map of India and two large Mycielski benchmark graphs with hidden minimum vertex colorings. In each case, the algorithm finds a proper m-coloring of the vertices of the graph G in polynomial-time with m equal to the chromatic number $\chi(G)$.

7.1. The Tetrahedron [8]. We run the program on the graph of the Tetrahedron with $n = 4$ vertices. The algorithm finds a proper m-coloring of the vertices for $m = \chi(G) = 4$.

```
graph.txt
4
0 1 1 1
1 0 1 1
1 1 0 1
1 1 1 0

coloring.txt
Vertex Coloring ( 4 ): ( 1 , 1 ) ( 2 , 2 ) ( 3 , 3 ) ( 4 , 4 )
```

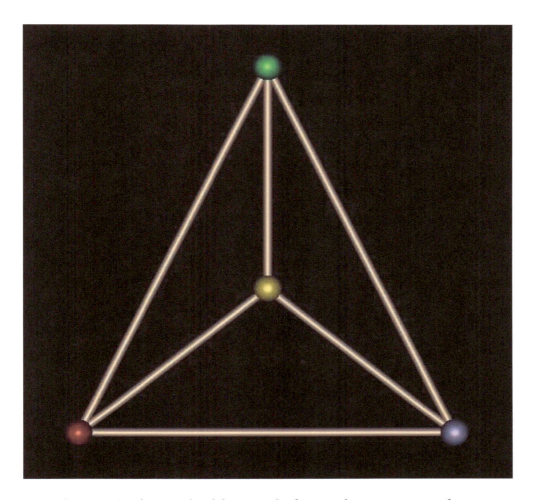

Figure 7.1. *The graph of the Tetrahedron with a proper m-coloring*
$(n = 4, m = \chi(G) = 4)$.

7.2. The Kuratowski Bipartite Graph $K_{3,3}$ [9]. We run the program on the Kuratowski bipartite graph $K_{3,3}$ with $n = 6$ vertices. The algorithm finds a proper m-coloring of the vertices for $m = \chi(G) = 2$.

graph.txt
```
6
0 0 0 1 1 1
0 0 0 1 1 1
0 0 0 1 1 1
1 1 1 0 0 0
1 1 1 0 0 0
1 1 1 0 0 0
```

coloring.txt
```
Vertex Coloring ( 6 ): ( 1 , 1 ) ( 2 , 1 ) ( 3 , 1 ) ( 4 , 2 )
( 5 , 2 ) ( 6 , 2 )
```

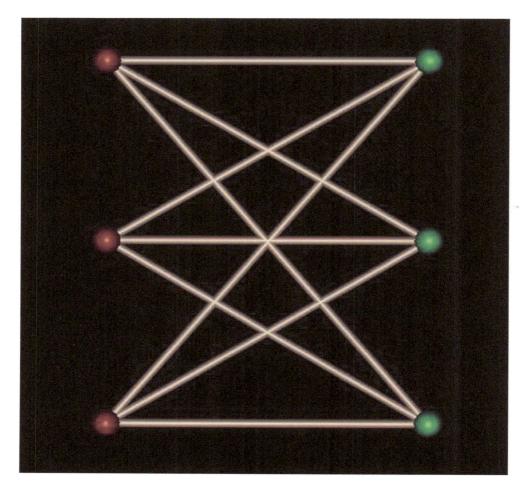

Figure 7.2. *The Kuratowski graph $K_{3,3}$ with a proper m-coloring*
($n = 6$, $m = \chi(G) = 2$).

7.3. The Octahedron [8]. We run the program on the graph of the Octahedron with $n = 6$ vertices. The algorithm finds a proper *m*-coloring of the vertices for $m = \chi(G) = 3$.

```
graph.txt
6
0 1 1 0 1 1
1 0 1 1 0 1
1 1 0 1 1 0
0 1 1 0 1 1
1 0 1 1 0 1
1 1 0 1 1 0


coloring.txt
Vertex Coloring ( 6 ): ( 1 , 1 ) ( 2 , 2 ) ( 3 , 3 ) ( 4 , 1 )
( 5 , 2 ) ( 6 , 3 )
```

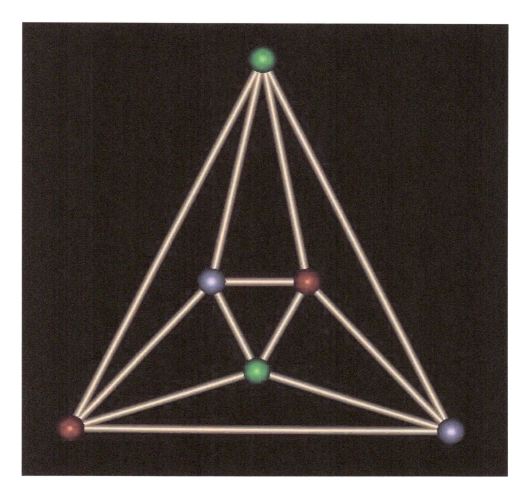

***Figure* 7.3.** *The graph of the Octahedron with a proper m-coloring*
($n = 6$, $m = \chi(G) = 3$).

7.4. The Bondy-Murty Graph G_1 [4]. We run the program on the Bondy-Murty graph G_1 with $n = 7$ vertices. The algorithm finds a proper m-coloring of the vertices for $m = \chi(G) = 4$.

graph.txt
```
7
0 1 1 0 1 1 0
1 0 1 1 0 1 0
1 1 0 1 1 0 0
0 1 1 0 0 0 1
1 0 1 0 0 0 1
1 1 0 0 0 0 1
0 0 0 1 1 1 0
```

coloring.txt
```
Vertex Coloring ( 7 ): ( 1 , 1 ) ( 2 , 2 ) ( 3 , 3 ) ( 4 , 1 )
( 5 , 2 ) ( 6 , 3 ) ( 7 , 4 )
```

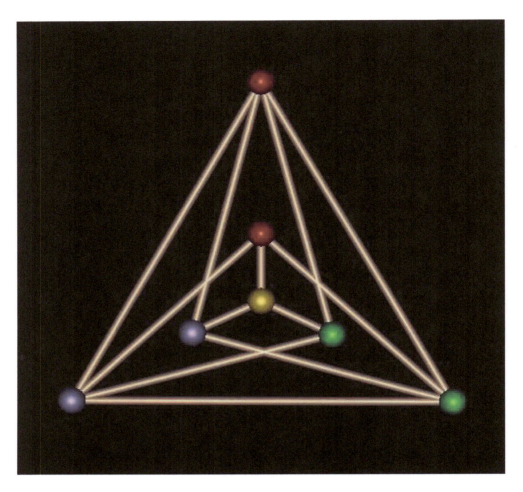

Figure 7.4. *The Bondy-Murty graph* G_1 *with a proper m-coloring*
$(\ n = 7,\ m = \chi(G) = 4\ )$.

7.5. The Wheel Graph W_8 [4]. We run the program on the Wheel graph W_8 with $n = 8$ vertices. The algorithm finds a proper *m*-coloring of the vertices for $m = \chi(G) = 4$.

graph.txt
```
8
0 1 0 0 0 0 1 1
1 0 1 0 0 0 0 1
0 1 0 1 0 0 0 1
0 0 1 0 1 0 0 1
0 0 0 1 0 1 0 1
0 0 0 0 1 0 1 1
1 0 0 0 0 1 0 1
1 1 1 1 1 1 1 0
```

coloring.txt
```
Vertex Coloring ( 8 ): ( 1 , 1 ) ( 2 , 2 ) ( 3 , 1 ) ( 4 , 2 )
( 5 , 1 ) ( 6 , 2 ) ( 7 , 3 ) ( 8 , 4 )
```

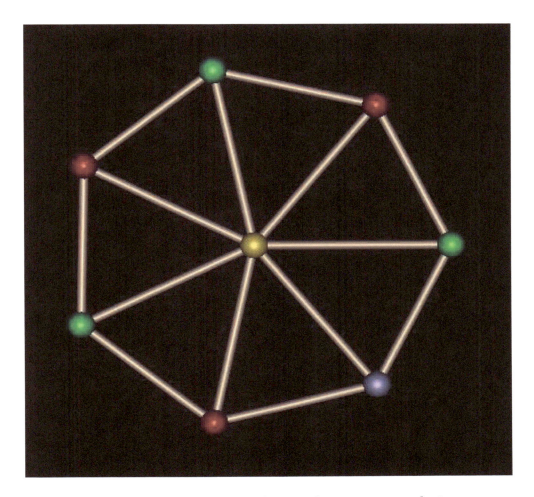

Figure 7.5. The Wheel graph W_8 with a proper m-coloring
($n = 8$, $m = \chi(G) = 4$).

7.6. The Cube [8]. We run the program on the graph of the Cube with $n = 8$ vertices. The algorithm finds a proper *m*-coloring of the vertices for $m = \chi(G) = 2$.

graph.txt
```
8
0 1 0 1 0 1 0 0
1 0 1 0 0 0 1 0
0 1 0 1 0 0 0 1
1 0 1 0 1 0 0 0
0 0 0 1 0 1 0 1
1 0 0 0 1 0 1 0
0 1 0 0 0 1 0 1
0 0 1 0 1 0 1 0
```

coloring.txt
```
Vertex Coloring ( 8 ): ( 1 , 1 ) ( 2 , 2 ) ( 3 , 1 ) ( 4 , 2 )
( 5 , 1 ) ( 6 , 2 ) ( 7 , 1 ) ( 8 , 2 )
```

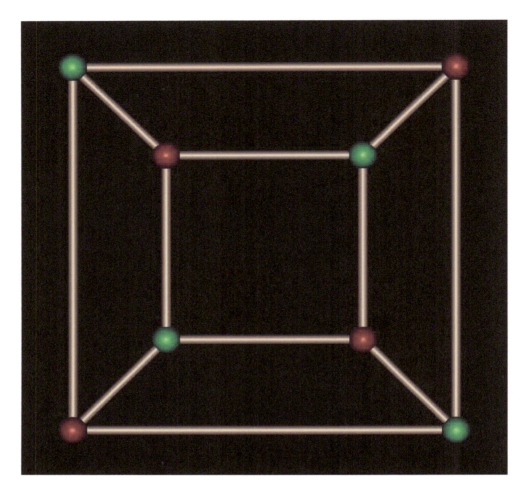

Figure 7.6. *The graph of the Cube with a proper m-coloring*
($n = 8$, $m = \chi(G) = 2$).

7.7. The Petersen Graph [10]. We run the program on the Petersen graph with $n = 10$ vertices. The algorithm finds a proper *m*-coloring of the vertices for $m = \chi(G) = 3$.

graph.txt
```
10
0 1 0 0 1 0 1 0 0 0
1 0 1 0 0 0 0 1 0 0
0 1 0 1 0 0 0 0 1 0
0 0 1 0 1 0 0 0 0 1
1 0 0 1 0 1 0 0 0 0
0 0 0 0 1 0 0 1 1 0
1 0 0 0 0 0 0 0 1 1
0 1 0 0 0 1 0 0 0 1
0 0 1 0 0 1 1 0 0 0
0 0 0 1 0 0 1 1 0 0
```

coloring.txt
```
Vertex Coloring ( 10 ): ( 1 , 1 ) ( 2 , 2 ) ( 3 , 1 ) ( 4 , 2 )
( 5 , 3 ) ( 6 , 1 ) ( 7 , 2 ) ( 8 , 3 ) ( 9 , 3 ) ( 10 , 1 )
```

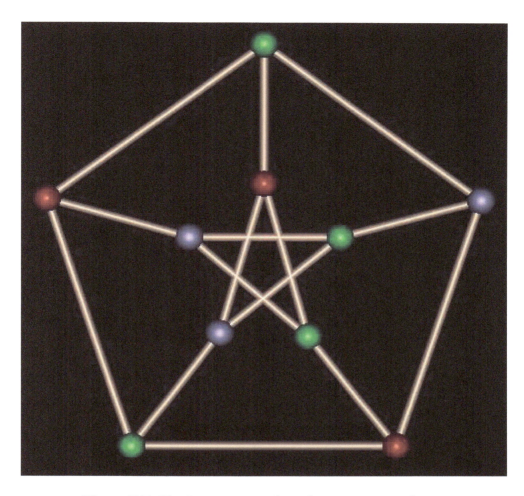

***Figure* 7.7.** *The Petersen graph with a proper m-coloring*
($n = 10$, $m = \chi(G) = 3$).

7.8. The Bondy-Murty graph G_2 [4]. We run the program on the Bondy-Murty graph G_2 with $n = 11$ vertices. The algorithm finds a proper m-coloring of the vertices for $m = \chi(G) = 3$.

graph.txt
```
11
0 0 1 1 1 1 0 1 1 1 1
0 0 1 1 1 1 0 1 1 1 1
1 1 0 1 0 0 1 0 0 0 0
1 1 1 0 0 0 1 0 0 0 0
1 1 0 0 0 1 1 0 0 0 0
1 1 0 0 1 0 1 0 0 0 0
0 0 1 1 1 1 0 1 1 1 1
1 1 0 0 0 0 1 0 1 0 0
1 1 0 0 0 0 1 1 0 0 0
1 1 0 0 0 0 1 0 0 0 1
1 1 0 0 0 0 1 0 0 1 0
```

coloring.txt
```
Vertex Coloring ( 11 ): ( 1 , 1 ) ( 2 , 1 ) ( 3 , 2 ) ( 4 , 3 )
```

35

```
( 5 , 2 ) ( 6 , 3 ) ( 7 , 1 ) ( 8 , 2 ) ( 9 , 3 ) ( 10 , 2 )
( 11 , 3 )
```

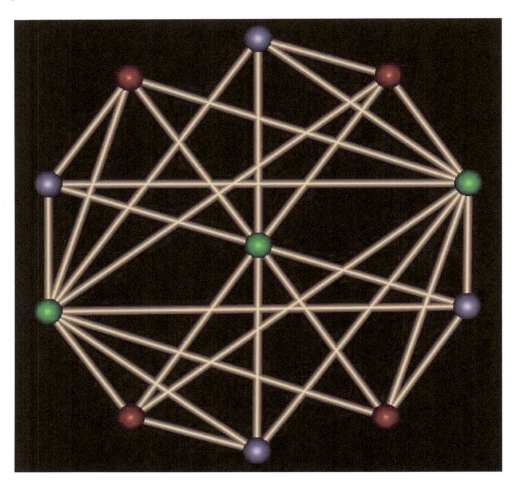

Figure 7.8. *The Bondy-Murty graph* G_2 *with a proper m-coloring*
($n = 11$, $m = \chi(G) = 3$).

7.9. The Grötzsch Graph [11]. We run the program on the Grötzsch graph with $n = 11$ vertices. The algorithm finds a proper *m*-coloring of the vertices for $m = \chi(G) = 4$.

graph.txt
```
11
0 1 1 1 1 1 0 0 0 0 0
1 0 0 0 0 0 1 0 1 0 0
1 0 0 0 0 0 0 1 0 1 0
1 0 0 0 0 0 0 0 1 0 1
1 0 0 0 0 0 1 0 0 1 0
1 0 0 0 0 0 0 1 0 0 1
0 1 0 0 1 0 0 1 0 0 1
0 0 1 0 0 1 1 0 1 0 0
0 1 0 1 0 0 0 1 0 1 0
0 0 1 0 1 0 0 0 1 0 1
0 0 0 1 0 1 0 1 1 0 1 0
```

```
coloring.txt
Vertex Coloring ( 11 ): ( 1 , 1 ) ( 2 , 2 ) ( 3 , 2 ) ( 4 , 2 )
( 5 , 2 ) ( 6 , 2 ) ( 7 , 1 ) ( 8 , 3 ) ( 9 , 1 ) ( 10 , 3 )
( 11 , 4 )
```

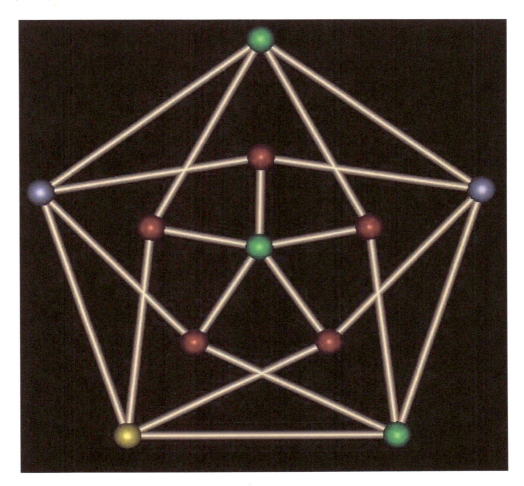

Figure 7.9. *The Grötzsch graph with a proper m-coloring*
($n = 11$, $m = \chi(G) = 4$).

7.10. The Chvátal Graph [12]. We run the program on the Chvátal graph with $n = 12$ vertices. The algorithm finds a proper *m*-coloring of the vertices for $m = \chi(G) = 4$.

graph.txt
```
12
0 1 0 0 1 0 1 0 0 1 0 0
1 0 1 0 0 1 0 1 0 1 0 0 0
0 1 0 1 0 0 1 0 1 0 1 0 0 0
0 0 1 0 1 0 0 1 0 1 0 1 0 0
1 0 0 1 0 1 0 0 1 0 0 0
0 1 0 0 1 0 0 0 0 1 0 1
1 0 1 0 0 0 0 0 0 0 1 1
0 1 0 1 0 0 0 0 0 0 1 1
0 0 1 0 1 0 0 0 0 0 1 1
1 0 0 1 0 1 0 0 0 0 1 0
```

37

```
0 0 0 0 0 0 1 1 1 1 0 0
0 0 0 0 0 1 1 1 1 0 0 0
```

coloring.txt
```
Vertex Coloring ( 12 ): ( 1 , 1 ) ( 2 , 2 ) ( 3 , 1 ) ( 4 , 2 )
( 5 , 3 ) ( 6 , 1 ) ( 7 , 3 ) ( 8 , 1 ) ( 9 , 4 ) ( 10 , 3 ) ( 11 , 2 )
( 12 , 2 )
```

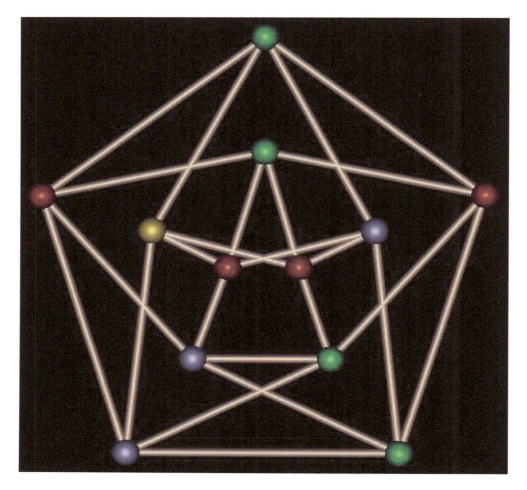

***Figure* 7.10.** *The Chvátal graph with a proper m-coloring*
($n = 12$, $m = \chi(G) = 4$).

7.11. The Icosahedron [8]. We run the program on the graph of the Icosahedron with $n = 12$ vertices. The algorithm finds a proper m-coloring of the vertices for $m = \chi(G) = 4$.

graph.txt
```
12
 0 1 1 0 0 1 1 1 0 0 0 0
 1 0 1 1 1 1 0 0 0 0 0 0
 1 1 0 1 0 0 0 0 1 1 0 0
 0 1 1 0 1 0 0 0 0 1 1 0 0
 0 1 0 1 0 1 0 0 0 0 1 1 0
 1 1 0 0 1 0 1 0 1 0 0 0 1 0
```

38

```
1 0 0 0 0 1 0 1 0 0 1 1
1 0 1 0 0 0 1 0 1 0 1 0 0 1
0 0 1 1 0 0 0 1 0 1 0 1
0 0 0 1 1 0 0 0 1 0 1 1
0 0 0 0 1 1 1 0 0 1 0 1
0 0 0 0 0 0 1 1 1 1 1 0
```

coloring.txt
```
Vertex Coloring ( 12 ): ( 1 , 3 ) ( 2 , 1 ) ( 3 , 2 ) ( 4 , 3 )
( 5 , 4 ) ( 6 , 2 ) ( 7 , 4 ) ( 8 , 1 ) ( 9 , 4 ) ( 10 , 1 ) ( 11 , 3 )
( 12 , 2 )
```

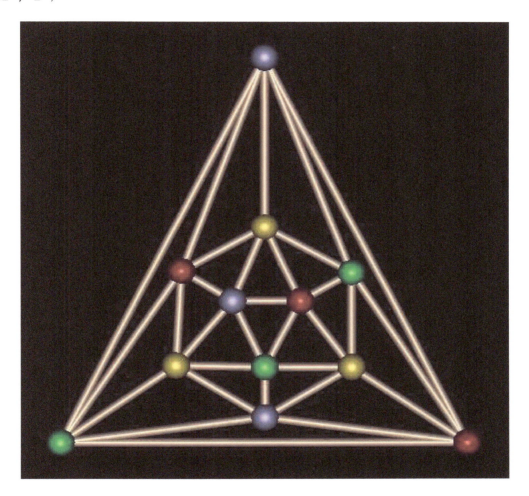

***Figure* 7.11.** *The graph of the Icosahedron with a proper m-coloring*
($n = 12$, $m = \chi(G) = 4$).

7.12. The Bondy-Murty graph G_3 [4]. We run the program on the Bondy-Murty graph G_3 with $n = 14$ vertices. The algorithm finds a proper m-coloring of the vertices for $m = \chi(G) = 2$.

graph.txt
```
14
0 0 0 1 0 0 0 1 0 0 0 1 0 0
```

```
0 0 1 0 0 0 1 0 0 0 1 0 0 0
0 1 0 1 0 0 0 0 0 0 0 0 0 1
1 0 1 0 1 0 0 0 0 0 0 0 0 0
0 0 0 1 0 1 0 0 0 1 0 0 0 0
0 0 0 0 1 0 1 0 0 0 0 0 1 0
0 1 0 0 0 1 0 1 0 0 0 0 0 0
1 0 0 0 0 0 1 0 1 0 0 0 0 0
0 0 0 0 0 0 0 1 0 1 0 0 0 1
0 0 0 0 1 0 0 0 1 0 1 0 0 0
0 1 0 0 0 0 0 0 0 1 0 1 0 0
1 0 0 0 0 0 0 0 0 0 1 0 1 0
0 0 0 0 0 1 0 0 0 0 0 1 0 1
0 0 1 0 0 0 0 0 1 0 0 0 1 0
```

coloring.txt
```
Vertex Coloring ( 14 ): ( 1 , 1 ) ( 2 , 2 ) ( 3 , 1 ) ( 4 , 2 )
( 5 , 1 ) ( 6 , 2 ) ( 7 , 1 ) ( 8 , 2 ) ( 9 , 1 ) ( 10 , 2 ) ( 11 , 1 )
( 12 , 2 ) ( 13 , 1 ) ( 14 , 2 )
```

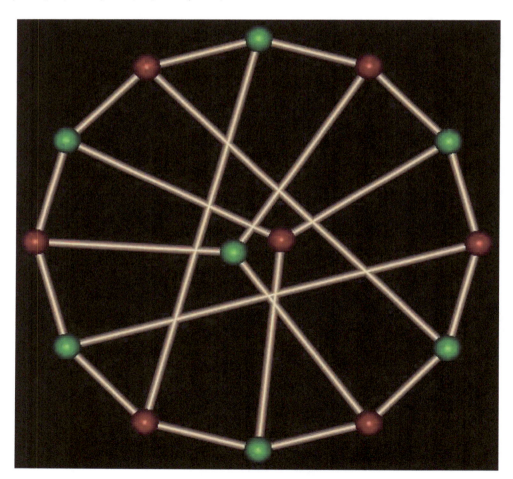

Figure 7.12. *The Bondy-Murty graph G₃ with a proper m-coloring*
($n = 14$, $m = \chi(G) = 2$).

7.13. The Bondy-Murty graph G_4 [4]. We run the program on the Bondy-Murty graph G_4 with $n = 16$ vertices. The algorithm finds a proper m-coloring of the vertices for $m = \chi(G) = 3$.

graph.txt
```
16
0 0 0 0 0 1 0 0 0 0 0 0 1 0 0 0
0 0 0 0 0 0 1 0 0 1 0 0 0 0 0 0
0 0 0 0 0 1 0 0 0 0 0 0 1 0 0 0
0 0 0 0 0 0 0 0 0 0 1 0 0 0 0 0
0 0 0 0 0 0 0 1 0 0 0 0 0 0 0 0
1 0 1 0 0 0 0 0 0 0 1 0 0 0 0 0
0 1 0 0 0 0 0 0 1 0 0 0 0 0 0 0
0 0 0 0 1 0 0 0 0 0 0 1 0 1 0 0
0 0 0 0 0 0 1 0 0 0 0 0 0 0 1 0
0 1 0 0 0 0 0 0 0 0 0 0 0 0 1 0
0 0 0 1 0 1 0 0 0 0 0 0 0 0 0 0
0 0 0 0 0 0 0 1 0 0 0 0 0 0 0 0
1 0 1 0 0 0 0 0 0 0 0 0 0 0 0 0
0 0 0 0 0 0 0 1 0 0 0 0 0 0 0 0
0 0 0 0 0 0 0 0 1 1 0 0 0 0 0 1
0 0 0 0 0 0 0 0 0 0 0 0 0 0 1 0
```

coloring.txt
```
Vertex Coloring ( 16 ): ( 1 , 1 ) ( 2 , 1 ) ( 3 , 1 ) ( 4 , 2 )
( 5 , 1 ) ( 6 , 2 ) ( 7 , 2 ) ( 8 , 2 ) ( 9 , 1 ) ( 10 , 2 ) ( 11 , 1 )
( 12 , 1 ) ( 13 , 2 ) ( 14 , 1 ) ( 15 , 3 ) ( 16 , 1 )
```

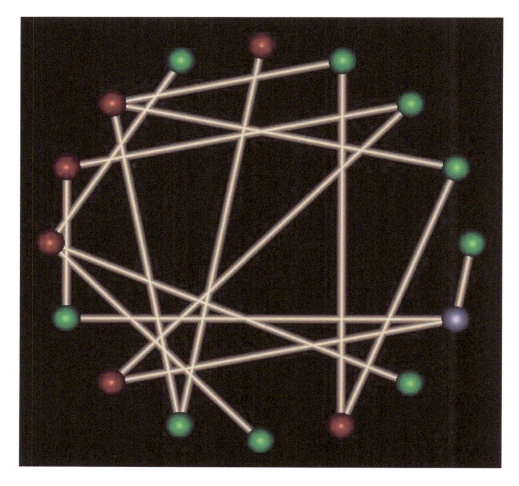

Figure 7.13. The Bondy-Murty graph G_4 with a proper m-coloring
($n = 16$, $m = \chi(G) = 3$).

7.14. The Ramsey Graph $R(4,4)$ [6]. We run the program on the Ramsey graph $R(4,4)$ with $n = 17$ vertices. The algorithm finds a proper m-coloring of the vertices for $m = \chi(G)$ = 6.

graph.txt
```
17
0 1 1 0 1 0 0 0 1 1 0 0 0 1 0 1 1
1 0 1 1 0 1 0 0 0 1 1 0 0 0 1 0 1
1 1 0 1 1 0 1 0 0 0 1 1 0 0 0 1 0
0 1 1 0 1 1 0 1 0 0 0 1 1 0 0 0 1
1 0 1 1 0 1 1 0 1 0 0 0 1 1 0 0 0
0 1 0 1 1 0 1 1 0 1 0 0 0 1 1 0 0
0 0 1 0 1 1 0 1 1 0 1 0 0 0 1 1 0
0 0 0 1 0 1 1 0 1 1 0 1 0 0 0 1 1
1 0 0 0 1 0 1 1 0 1 1 0 1 0 0 0 1
1 1 0 0 0 1 0 1 1 0 1 1 0 1 0 0 0
0 1 1 0 0 0 1 0 1 1 0 1 1 0 1 0 0
0 0 1 1 0 0 0 1 0 1 1 0 1 1 0 1 0
0 0 0 1 1 0 0 0 1 0 1 1 0 1 1 0 1
1 0 0 0 1 1 0 0 0 1 0 1 1 0 1 1 0
```

```
0 1 0 0 0 1 1 0 0 0 1 0 1 1 0 1 1
1 0 1 0 0 0 1 1 0 0 0 1 0 1 1 1 0 1
1 1 0 1 0 0 0 1 1 0 0 0 1 0 1 1 0
```

coloring.txt
```
Vertex Coloring ( 17 ): ( 1 , 2 ) ( 2 , 1 ) ( 3 , 3 ) ( 4 , 4 )
( 5 , 1 ) ( 6 , 2 ) ( 7 , 6 ) ( 8 , 5 ) ( 9 , 4 ) ( 10 , 3 ) ( 11 , 2 )
( 12 , 6 ) ( 13 , 5 ) ( 14 , 4 ) ( 15 , 3 ) ( 16 , 1 ) ( 17 , 6 )
```

Figure 7.14. The Ramsey graph R(4,4) with a proper m-coloring
$$(n = 17, m = \chi(G) = 6).$$

7.15. The Dodecahedron [8]. We run the program on the graph of the Dodecahedron with $n = 20$ vertices. The algorithm finds a proper *m*-coloring of the vertices for $m = \chi(G) = 3$.

graph.txt
```
20
0 1 0 0 1 0 0 0 0 0 0 0 0 0 0 1 0 0 0 0
1 0 1 0 0 0 0 0 0 0 0 0 1 0 0 0 0 0 0 0
0 1 0 1 0 0 0 0 0 1 0 0 0 0 0 0 0 0 0 0
0 0 1 0 1 0 0 1 0 0 0 0 0 0 0 0 0 0 0 0
1 0 0 1 0 1 0 1 0 0 0 0 0 0 0 0 0 0 0 0
```

43

```
0 0 0 0 1 0 1 0 0 0 0 0 0 0 0 1 0 0 0 0 0
0 0 0 0 0 1 0 1 0 0 0 0 0 0 0 0 0 1 0 0 0
0 0 0 1 0 0 1 0 1 0 0 0 0 0 0 0 0 0 0 0 0
0 0 0 0 0 0 0 1 0 1 0 0 0 0 0 0 0 1 0 0
0 0 1 0 0 0 0 0 1 0 1 0 0 0 0 0 0 0 0 0 0
0 0 0 0 0 0 0 0 0 1 0 1 0 0 0 0 0 0 1 0
0 1 0 0 0 0 0 0 0 0 1 0 1 0 0 0 0 0 0 0 0
0 0 0 0 0 0 0 0 0 0 0 1 0 1 0 0 0 0 0 1
1 0 0 0 0 0 0 0 0 0 0 0 1 0 1 0 0 0 0 0
0 0 0 0 0 1 0 0 0 0 0 0 0 1 0 1 0 0 0 0
0 0 0 0 0 0 0 0 0 0 0 0 0 0 1 0 1 0 0 1
0 0 0 0 0 0 1 0 0 0 0 0 0 0 0 1 0 1 0 0
0 0 0 0 0 0 0 0 1 0 0 0 0 0 0 0 1 0 1 0
0 0 0 0 0 0 0 0 0 0 1 0 0 0 0 0 0 1 0 1
0 0 0 0 0 0 0 0 0 0 0 1 0 0 1 0 0 1 0
```

coloring.txt
```
Vertex Coloring ( 20 ): ( 1 , 2 ) ( 2 , 3 ) ( 3 , 1 ) ( 4 , 2 )
( 5 , 3 ) ( 6 , 1 ) ( 7 , 2 ) ( 8 , 3 ) ( 9 , 2 ) ( 10 , 3 ) ( 11 , 2 )
( 12 , 1 ) ( 13 , 3 ) ( 14 , 1 ) ( 15 , 3 ) ( 16 , 2 ) ( 17 , 3 )
( 18 , 1 ) ( 19 , 3 ) ( 20 , 1 )
```

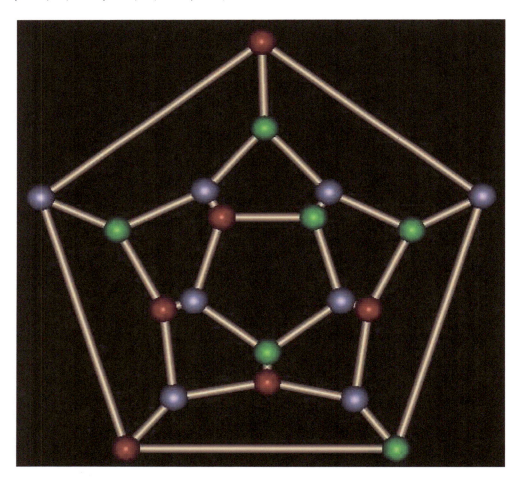

***Figure* 7.15.** *The graph of the Dodecahedron with a proper m-coloring*
($n = 20$, $m = \chi(G) = 3$).

7.16. The Mycielski 5-Chromatic Graph [13]. We run the program on the Mycielski 5-chromatic graph with $n = 23$ vertices. The algorithm finds a proper m-coloring of the vertices for $m = \chi(G) = 5$.

graph.txt
```
23
0 1 0 1 0 0 1 0 1 0 0 0 1 0 1 0 0 1 0 1 0 0 0
1 0 1 0 0 1 0 1 0 0 0 1 0 1 0 0 1 0 1 0 0 0 0
0 1 0 0 1 0 1 0 0 1 0 0 1 0 0 1 0 1 0 0 1 0 0
1 0 0 0 1 1 0 0 0 1 0 1 0 0 0 1 1 0 0 0 1 0 0
0 0 1 1 0 0 0 1 1 0 0 0 0 1 1 0 0 0 1 1 0 0 0
0 1 0 1 0 0 0 0 0 0 1 0 1 0 1 0 0 0 0 0 0 1 0
1 0 1 0 0 0 0 0 0 0 1 1 0 1 0 0 0 0 0 0 0 1 0
0 1 0 0 1 0 0 0 0 0 1 0 1 0 0 1 0 0 0 0 0 1 0
1 0 0 0 1 0 0 0 0 0 1 1 0 0 0 1 0 0 0 0 0 1 0
0 0 1 1 0 0 0 0 0 0 1 0 0 1 1 0 0 0 0 0 0 1 0
0 0 0 0 0 1 1 1 1 1 0 0 0 0 0 0 1 1 1 1 1 0 0
0 1 0 1 0 0 1 0 1 0 0 0 0 0 0 0 0 0 0 0 0 0 1
1 0 1 0 0 1 0 1 0 0 0 0 0 0 0 0 0 0 0 0 0 0 1
0 1 0 0 1 0 1 0 0 1 0 0 0 0 0 0 0 0 0 0 0 0 1
1 0 0 0 1 1 0 0 0 1 0 0 0 0 0 0 0 0 0 0 0 0 1
0 0 1 1 0 0 0 1 1 0 0 0 0 0 0 0 0 0 0 0 0 0 1
0 1 0 1 0 0 0 0 0 0 1 0 0 0 0 0 0 0 0 0 0 0 1
1 0 1 0 0 0 0 0 0 0 1 0 0 0 0 0 0 0 0 0 0 0 1
0 1 0 0 1 0 0 0 0 0 1 0 0 0 0 0 0 0 0 0 0 0 1
1 0 0 0 1 0 0 0 0 0 1 0 0 0 0 0 0 0 0 0 0 0 1
0 0 1 1 0 0 0 0 0 0 1 0 0 0 0 0 0 0 0 0 0 0 1
0 0 0 0 0 1 1 1 1 1 0 0 0 0 0 0 0 0 0 0 0 0 1
0 0 0 0 0 0 0 0 0 0 0 1 1 1 1 1 1 1 1 1 1 1 0
```

coloring.txt
```
Vertex Coloring ( 23 ): ( 1 , 1 ) ( 2 , 2 ) ( 3 , 1 ) ( 4 , 2 )
( 5 , 3 ) ( 6 , 1 ) ( 7 , 2 ) ( 8 , 1 ) ( 9 , 2 ) ( 10 , 3 ) ( 11 , 4 )
( 12 , 1 ) ( 13 , 2 ) ( 14 , 1 ) ( 15 , 2 ) ( 16 , 3 ) ( 17 , 1 )
( 18 , 2 ) ( 19 , 1 ) ( 20 , 2 ) ( 21 , 3 ) ( 22 , 4 ) ( 23 , 5 )
```

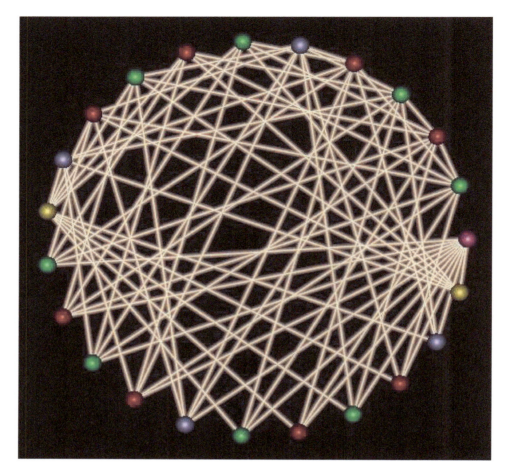

Figure 7.16. *The Mycielski 5-chromatic graph with a proper m-coloring* ($n = 23$, $m = \chi(G) = 5$).

7.17. The Grünbaum Graph [12]. We run the program on the Grünbaum graph with $n = 25$ vertices. The algorithm finds a proper m-coloring of the vertices for $m = \chi(G) = 4$.

graph.txt

```
25
0 1 0 0 0 0 0 0 0 1 0 1 0 0 0 0 0 0 0 0 0 0 1 0 0
1 0 1 0 0 0 0 0 0 0 0 0 1 0 0 0 0 0 0 0 0 1 0 0 0
0 1 0 1 0 0 0 0 0 0 0 0 0 1 0 0 0 0 0 0 0 0 0 1 0
0 0 1 0 1 0 0 0 0 0 0 0 0 0 1 0 0 0 0 0 0 0 1 0 0
0 0 0 1 0 1 0 0 0 0 0 0 0 0 0 1 0 0 0 0 0 0 0 0 1
0 0 0 0 1 0 1 0 0 0 0 0 0 0 0 0 1 0 0 0 0 0 0 1 0
0 0 0 0 0 1 0 1 0 0 0 0 0 0 0 0 0 1 0 0 1 0 0 0 0
0 0 0 0 0 0 1 0 1 0 0 0 0 0 0 0 0 0 1 0 0 0 0 0 1
0 0 0 0 0 0 0 1 0 1 0 0 0 0 0 0 0 0 0 1 0 1 0 0 0
1 0 0 0 0 0 0 0 1 0 1 0 0 0 0 0 0 0 0 0 0 1 0 0 0
0 0 0 0 0 0 0 0 0 1 0 0 1 0 0 0 0 1 0 0 0 0 1 0 0
1 0 0 0 0 0 0 0 0 0 0 0 1 0 0 0 0 0 1 0 0 0 0 0 1
0 1 0 0 0 0 0 0 0 0 1 0 0 0 1 0 0 0 0 0 0 0 0 0 1
0 0 1 0 0 0 0 0 0 0 0 1 0 0 0 1 0 0 0 0 1 0 0 0 0
0 0 0 1 0 0 0 0 0 0 0 0 1 0 0 0 1 0 0 0 1 0 0 0 0
0 0 0 0 1 0 0 0 0 0 0 0 0 1 0 0 0 1 0 0 0 1 0 0 0
```

```
0 0 0 0 0 1 0 0 0 0 0 0 0 0 1 0 0 0 1 0 0 1 0 0 0
0 0 0 0 0 0 1 0 0 0 0 0 0 0 0 1 0 0 0 1 0 0 1 0 0
0 0 0 0 0 0 0 1 0 0 1 0 0 0 0 0 1 0 0 0 0 0 1 0 0
0 0 0 0 0 0 0 0 1 0 0 1 0 0 0 0 0 1 0 0 0 0 0 1 0
0 0 0 0 0 0 1 0 0 1 0 0 0 1 1 0 0 0 0 0 0 0 0 0 0
0 1 0 0 0 0 0 0 1 0 0 0 0 0 0 1 1 0 0 0 0 0 0 0 0
1 0 0 1 0 0 0 0 0 0 0 0 0 0 0 0 0 1 1 0 0 0 0 0 0
0 0 1 0 0 1 0 0 0 0 1 0 0 0 0 0 0 0 0 1 0 0 0 0 0
0 0 0 0 1 0 0 1 0 0 0 1 1 0 0 0 0 0 0 0 0 0 0 0 0
```

coloring.txt
Vertex Coloring (25): (1 , 1) (2 , 2) (3 , 1) (4 , 2)
(5 , 1) (6 , 2) (7 , 3) (8 , 2) (9 , 1) (10 , 2) (11 , 3)
(12 , 2) (13 , 1) (14 , 3) (15 , 3) (16 , 2) (17 , 1)
(18 , 1) (19 , 4) (20 , 3) (21 , 1) (22 , 3) (23 , 3)
(24 , 4) (25 , 3)

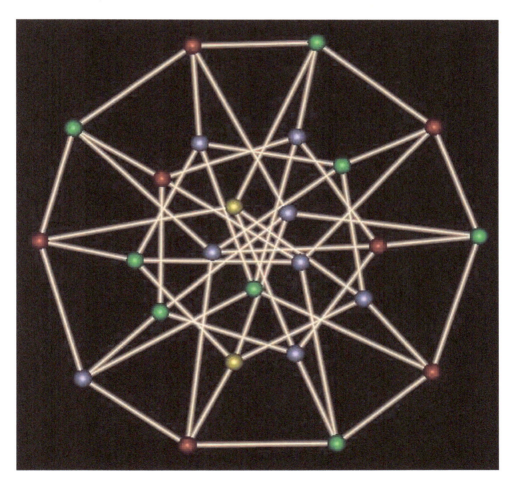

Figure 7.17. *The Grünbaum graph with a proper m-coloring*
($n = 25$, $m = \chi(G) = 4$).

7.18. The Map of India [14]. The 30 states of mainland India are shown below in Figure 7.18.1. We define the graph of India as follows. There is a unique vertex inside each region defined by a state. There is an edge connecting two distinct vertices if and only if the two corresponding regions have a whole segment of their boundaries in common. The graph of India is shown below in Figure 7.18.2. We run the program on the graph of India with $n = 30$ vertices. The algorithm finds a proper m-coloring of the vertices for $m = \chi(G) = 4$, and correspondingly, a proper four-coloring of the map of India.

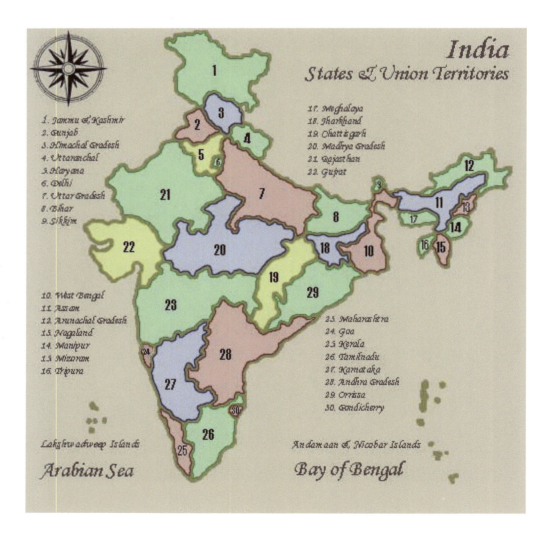

***Figure* 7.18.1.** *The Map of India with a proper four-coloring of its 30 mainland states.*

48

graph.txt
```
30
0 1 1 0 0 0 0 0 0 0 0 0 0 0 0 0 0 0 0 0 C 0 0 0 0 0 0 0 0 0
1 0 1 0 1 0 0 0 0 0 0 0 0 0 0 0 0 0 0 1 C 0 0 0 0 0 0 0 0 0
1 1 0 1 1 0 1 0 0 0 0 0 0 0 0 0 0 0 0 0 C 0 0 0 0 0 0 0 0 0
0 0 1 0 1 0 1 0 0 0 0 0 0 0 0 0 0 0 0 0 C 0 0 0 0 0 0 0 0 0
0 1 1 1 0 1 1 0 0 0 0 0 0 0 0 0 0 0 0 1 C 0 0 0 0 0 0 0 0 0
0 0 0 0 1 0 1 0 0 0 0 0 0 0 0 0 0 0 0 0 C 0 0 0 0 0 0 0 0 0
0 0 1 1 1 1 0 1 0 0 0 0 0 0 0 0 1 1 1 1 C 0 0 0 0 0 0 0 0 0
0 0 0 0 0 1 0 0 1 0 0 0 0 0 0 1 0 0 0 0 C 0 0 0 0 0 0 0 0 0
0 0 0 0 0 0 0 1 0 0 0 0 0 0 0 0 0 0 0 0 C 0 0 0 0 0 0 0 0 0
0 0 0 0 0 0 1 1 0 1 0 0 0 0 0 1 0 0 0 0 C 0 0 0 0 0 0 0 1 0
0 0 0 0 0 0 0 0 1 0 1 1 1 1 1 1 0 0 0 0 C 0 0 0 0 0 0 0 0 0
0 0 0 0 0 0 0 0 0 1 0 1 0 0 0 0 0 0 0 0 C 0 0 0 0 0 0 0 0 0
0 0 0 0 0 0 0 0 0 1 1 0 1 0 0 0 0 0 0 0 C 0 0 0 0 0 0 0 0 0
0 0 0 0 0 0 0 0 0 1 0 1 0 1 0 0 0 0 0 0 C 0 0 0 0 0 0 0 0 0
0 0 0 0 0 0 0 0 0 1 0 0 1 0 1 0 0 0 0 0 C 0 0 0 0 0 0 0 0 0
0 0 0 0 0 0 0 1 0 1 0 0 0 0 0 0 0 0 0 0 C 0 0 0 0 0 0 0 0 0
0 0 0 0 0 1 1 0 1 0 0 0 0 0 0 1 0 0 0 0 C 0 0 0 0 0 0 0 1 0
0 0 0 0 0 1 0 0 0 0 0 0 0 0 0 1 0 1 0 0 1 0 1 0 0 1 1 0 0 0
0 0 0 0 0 1 0 0 0 0 0 0 0 0 0 1 0 1 1 1 C 0 0 0 0 0 0 0 0 0
0 1 0 0 1 0 1 0 0 0 0 0 0 0 0 0 1 0 1 0 C 0 0 0 0 0 0 0 0 0
0 0 0 0 0 0 0 0 0 0 0 0 0 0 0 0 1 1 C 1 0 0 0 0 0 0 0 0 0 0
0 0 0 0 0 0 0 0 0 0 0 0 0 0 0 0 1 1 0 1 0 1 0 0 1 1 0 0 0 0
0 0 0 0 0 0 0 0 0 0 0 0 0 0 0 0 0 0 C 1 0 0 0 0 1 0 0 0 0 0
0 0 0 0 0 0 0 0 0 0 0 0 0 0 0 0 0 0 C 0 0 0 1 1 0 0 0 0 0 0
0 0 0 0 0 0 0 0 0 0 0 0 0 0 0 0 0 0 C 0 0 1 0 1 1 0 1 0 0 0
0 0 0 0 0 0 0 0 0 0 0 0 0 0 0 0 0 0 C 1 1 1 1 0 1 0 0 0 0 0
0 0 0 0 0 0 0 0 0 1 0 0 0 0 0 0 1 0 0 C 1 0 0 1 1 0 1 0 0 0
0 0 0 0 0 0 0 0 0 1 0 0 0 0 0 0 1 1 0 0 C 0 0 0 0 0 1 0 0 0
0 0 0 0 0 0 0 0 0 0 0 0 0 0 0 0 0 0 C 0 0 0 1 0 0 0 0 1 0 0
0 0 0 0 0 0 0 0 0 0 0 0 0 0 0 0 0 0 C 0 0 0 1 0 0 0 0 0 0 0
```

coloring.txt
```
Vertex Coloring ( 30 ): ( 1 , 1 ) ( 2 , 2 ) ( 3 , 3 ) ( 4 , 1 )
( 5 , 4 ) ( 6 , 1 ) ( 7 , 2 ) ( 8 , 1 ) ( 9 , 1 ) ( 10 , 2 ) ( 11 , 3 )
( 12 , 1 ) ( 13 , 2 ) ( 14 , 1 ) ( 15 , 2 ) ( 16 , 1 ) ( 17 , 1 )
( 18 , 3 ) ( 19 , 4 ) ( 20 , 3 ) ( 21 , 1 ) ( 22 , 4 ) ( 23 , 1 )
( 24 , 2 ) ( 25 , 2 ) ( 26 , 1 ) ( 27 , 3 ) ( 28 , 2 ) ( 29 , 1 )
( 30 , 2 )
```

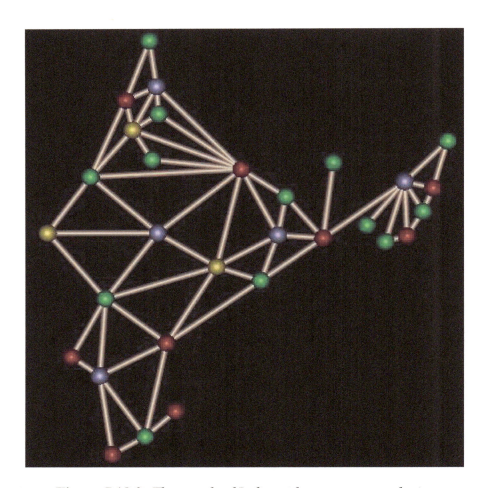

Figure 7.18.2. *The graph of India with a proper m-coloring*
($n = 30$, $m = \chi(G) = 4$).

7.19. The Mycielski 6-Chromatic Graph [13]. We run the program on the Mycielski 6-chromatic graph with $n = 47$ vertices. The algorithm finds a proper m-coloring of the vertices for $m = \chi(G) = 6$.

graph.txt
[download]

coloring.txt
```
Vertex Coloring ( 47 ): ( 1 , 1 ) ( 2 , 2 ) ( 3 , 1 ) ( 4 , 2 )
( 5 , 3 ) ( 6 , 1 ) ( 7 , 2 ) ( 8 , 1 ) ( 9 , 2 ) ( 10 , 3 ) ( 11 , 4 )
( 12 , 1 ) ( 13 , 2 ) ( 14 , 1 ) ( 15 , 2 ) ( 16 , 3 ) ( 17 , 1 )
( 18 , 2 ) ( 19 , 1 ) ( 20 , 2 ) ( 21 , 3 ) ( 22 , 4 ) ( 23 , 5 )
( 24 , 1 ) ( 25 , 2 ) ( 26 , 1 ) ( 27 , 2 ) ( 28 , 3 ) ( 29 , 1 )
( 30 , 2 ) ( 31 , 1 ) ( 32 , 2 ) ( 33 , 3 ) ( 34 , 4 ) ( 35 , 1 )
( 36 , 2 ) ( 37 , 1 ) ( 38 , 2 ) ( 39 , 3 ) ( 40 , 1 ) ( 41 , 2 )
( 42 , 1 ) ( 43 , 2 ) ( 44 , 3 ) ( 45 , 4 ) ( 46 , 5 ) ( 47 , 6 )
```

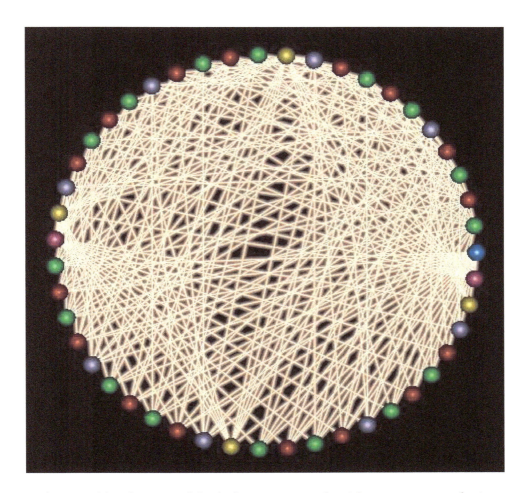

Figure 7.19. *The Mycielski 6-chromatic graph with a proper m-coloring*
(n = 47, m = χ(G) = 6).

7.20. The Mycielski 7-Chromatic Graph [13].
We run the program on the Mycielski 7-chromatic graph with $n = 95$ vertices. The algorithm finds a proper m-coloring of the vertices for $m = \chi(G) = 7$.

graph.txt
[download]

coloring.txt
```
Vertex Coloring ( 95 ): ( 1 , 1 ) ( 2 , 2 ) ( 3 , 1 ) ( 4 , 2 )
( 5 , 3 ) ( 6 , 1 ) ( 7 , 2 ) ( 8 , 1 ) ( 9 , 2 ) ( 10 , 3 ) ( 11 , 4 )
( 12 , 1 ) ( 13 , 2 ) ( 14 , 1 ) ( 15 , 2 ) ( 16 , 3 ) ( 17 , 1 )
( 18 , 2 ) ( 19 , 1 ) ( 20 , 2 ) ( 21 , 3 ) ( 22 , 4 ) ( 23 , 5 )
( 24 , 1 ) ( 25 , 2 ) ( 26 , 1 ) ( 27 , 2 ) ( 28 , 3 ) ( 29 , 1 )
( 30 , 2 ) ( 31 , 1 ) ( 32 , 2 ) ( 33 , 3 ) ( 34 , 4 ) ( 35 , 1 )
( 36 , 2 ) ( 37 , 1 ) ( 38 , 2 ) ( 39 , 3 ) ( 40 , 1 ) ( 41 , 2 )
( 42 , 1 ) ( 43 , 2 ) ( 44 , 3 ) ( 45 , 4 ) ( 46 , 5 ) ( 47 , 6 )
( 48 , 1 ) ( 49 , 2 ) ( 50 , 1 ) ( 51 , 2 ) ( 52 , 3 ) ( 53 , 1 )
( 54 , 2 ) ( 55 , 1 ) ( 56 , 2 ) ( 57 , 3 ) ( 58 , 4 ) ( 59 , 1 )
( 60 , 2 ) ( 61 , 1 ) ( 62 , 2 ) ( 63 , 3 ) ( 64 , 1 ) ( 65 , 2 )
( 66 , 1 ) ( 67 , 2 ) ( 68 , 3 ) ( 69 , 4 ) ( 70 , 5 ) ( 71 , 1 )
```

(72 , 2) (73 , 1) (74 , 2) (75 , 3) (76 , 1) (77 , 2)
(78 , 1) (79 , 2) (80 , 3) (81 , 4) (82 , 1) (83 , 2)
(84 , 1) (85 , 2) (86 , 3) (87 , 1) (88 , 2) (89 , 1)
(90 , 2) (91 , 3) (92 , 4) (93 , 5) (94 , 6) (95 , 7)

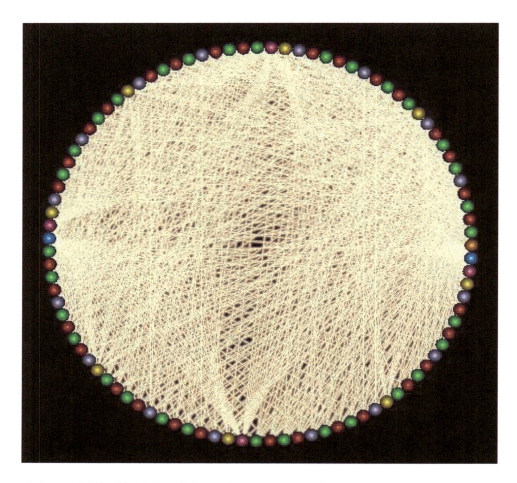

Figure 7.20. *The Mycielski 7-chromatic graph with a proper m-coloring*
($n = 95$, $m = \chi(G) = 7$).

8. References

[1]   R.M. Karp, *Reducibility among combinatorial problems*, Complexity of Computer Computations, Plenum Press, 1972.

[2]   R. Frucht, *Graphs of degree three with a given abstract group*, Canad. J. Math., 1949.

[3]   Stephen Cook, *The **P** versus **NP** Problem*, Official Problem Description, Millennium Problems, Clay Mathematics Institute, 2000.

[4]   J.A. Bondy and U.S.R. Murty, *Graph Theory with Applications*, Elsevier Science Publishing Co., Inc, 1976.

[5]   Euclid, *Elements*, circa 300 B.C.

[6]   F.P. Ramsey, *On a problem of formal logic*, Proc. London Math. Soc., 1930.

[7]   Stanley Lippman, *Essential C++*, Addison-Wesley, 2000.

[8]   Plato, *Timaeaus*, circa 350 B.C.

[9]   K. Kuratowski, *Sur le problème des courbes gauches en topologie*, Fund. Math., 1930.

[10] J. Petersen, *Die Theorie der regulären Graphen*, Acta Math., 1891.

[11] H. Grötzsch, *Ein Dreifarbensatz für dreikreisfreie Netz auf der Kugel*, Z. Martin-Luther-Univ., 1958.

[12] B. Grünbaum, *A Problem in Graph Coloring*, Amer. Math. Monthly, 1970.

[13] J. Mycielski, *Sur le coloriage des graphs*, Colloq. Math., 1955.

[14] Ashay Dharwadker, *A New Proof of the Four Colour Theorem*, **http://www.dharwadker.org** , 2000.

[15] C. Berge, *Graphes et Hypergraphes*, Dunod, 1970.

[16] Ashay Dharwadker, *The Vertex Cover Algorithm*, **http://www.dharwadker.org/vertex_cover** , 2006.

[17] Ashay Dharwadker, *The Independent Set Algorithm*, **http://www.dharwadker.org/independent_set** , 2006.

[18] Ashay Dharwadker, *The Clique Algorithm*, **http://www.dharwadker.org/clique** , 2006.

www.ingramcontent.com/pod-product-compliance
Lightning Source LLC
Chambersburg PA
CBHW041423050326

40689CB00002B/629